Eric Overmyer

NATIVE SPEECH

BROADWAY PLAY PUBLISHING INC.

357 W 20th St., NY NY 10011
212 627-1055

NATIVE SPEECH

First printing: July 1984
Second printing: March 1987

ISBN: 0-88145-017-0

Design by Marie Donovan
Set in Baskerville by L&F Technical Composition, Lakeland, FL
Printed on acid-free paper and bound by BookCrafters, Inc., Chelsea, MI

For

Melissa Cooper

NATIVE SPEECH received its professional premiere at The Los Angeles Actors Theatre, Bill Bushnell Producing/Artistic Director. The production was directed by John Olon, and produced by Diane White and Adam Leipzig.

The revised version of NATIVE SPEECH was first presented February 14, 1985 at Center Stage, Baltimore, with Stan Wojewodski, Artistic Director, Peter Culman, Managing Director, and the following cast:

HUNGRY MOTHER	Kario Salem
FREE LANCE	Lorey Hayes
BELLY UP	SáMi Chester
CHARLIE SAMOA	Khin-Kyaw Maung
JOHNNIE SUCROSE	Tzi Ma
JIMMY SHILLELAGH	Robert Salas
JANIS	Caris Corfman
THE MOOK	Samuel L. Jackson
HOOVER	Jimmy Smits
FREDDY NAVAJO/LOUD SPEAKER	Melinda Mallari
CRAZY JOE NAVAJO	Adam Gish

The production was directed by Paul Berman. Set Design was by Hugh Landwehr; Costumes, Jess Goldstein; Lights, Jim Ingalls; and Sound, Janet Kalas.

"If he was not as dead as the cold lasagna on which the tomato sauce has begun to darken, I was a Dutchman. The gaudy and, in the absence of blood, inappropriate metaphor actually came to mind at the moment, as a willed ruse to lure me away from panic—the fundamental purpose of most caprices of language, hence the American wisecrack."

Thomas Berger, *Who is Teddy Villanova?*

CHARACTERS
(in order of appearance)

HUNGRY MOTHER
LOUD SPEAKER (a woman's voice)
FREE LANCE*
BELLY UP
CHARLIE SAMOA
JOHNNIE SUCROSE (a transvestite)
JIMMY SHILLELAGH
JANIS*
THE MOOK
HOOVER
FREDDY NAVAJO*
CRAZY JOE NAVAJO

*women

Notes: HUNGRY MOTHER and JANIS are white. THE MOOK and FREE LANCE are black. They are an impressive, attractive couple: a Renaissance prince and princess. BELLY UP is black, middle-aged (somewhat older than HUNGRY MOTHER), a large man, an ex-sarge; the outline of his chevrons is still visible on his fatigue jacket. HOOVER, FREDDY NAVAJO, CRAZY JOE NAVAJO, CHARLIE SAMOA, JOHNNIE, and JIMMY should be played by Asian-American, Hispanic, or Native American actors.

FREDDY NAVAJO is a woman. LOUD SPEAKER is an unseen, amplified, *live* voice: one of those ubiquitous, bland women's voices heard in airports, shopping malls, or on the time of day recordings. LOUD SPEAKER can be doubled, but care should be taken to alter the voice so that the audience does not identify it with the onstage character.

JOHNNIE SUCROSE is a transvestite, a convincing one. The drag should be accomplished.

The following parts can be doubled:
    FREDDY and LOUD SPEAKER
    JIMMY and CRAZY JOE

This reduces the cast from 12 to 10. Doubling is not preferable, so care should be taken to make clear that doubling is an economic, not aesthetic choice.

Except where indicated, HUNGRY MOTHER's voice is *not* amplified during his broadcast monologues. We hear his voice as he hears it, not as it is heard over the radio by his listeners.

SETTING

HUNGRY MOTHER's underground radio station, and the devastated neighborhood which surrounds it.

The studio is constructed from the detritus of Western Civ: appliances, neon tubing, 45's, car parts. Junk.

Outside, a darkening world. Dangerous. The light is blue and chill. Always winter.

The time of the play is Now.

ACT ONE

(*The Studio.* HUNGRY MOTHER. *Red lights blinking in the black. A needle scrapes across a record. A low hum. Hum builds: the Konelrad Civil Defense Signal.* HUNGRY MOTHER *bops with the tone, scats with it. The tone builds, breaks off. Silence.* HUNGRY MOTHER *leans over the mike, says in a so-good-it-hurts voice:*)

HUNGRY MOTHER: O, that's a hit. Hungry Mother plays the hits, only the hits. I want some seafood, mama. (*Beat.*) This is your Hungry Mother here — and you know it.

(*Lights.* HUNGRY MOTHER *is a shambly, disheveled man in his late thirties. The Broadcast Indicator — a blue light bulb on the mike — is 'on'. And so is* HUNGRY MOTHER.)

HUNGRY MOTHER: (*Cooool.*) Static. Dead air. Can't beat it. With a stick. Audio entropy. In-creases ever-y-where. Home to roost. Crack a six-pack of that ambient sound. (*Beat.*) You've been groovin' and duckin' to the ever-popular sound of "Air Raid" — by Victor Chinaman. Moan with the tone. A blast from the past. With vocal variations by yours truly. The Hungry Mother. (*Beat.*) Hard enough for you? (*A little more up tempo.*) Hungry Mother here, your argot argonaut. Stick with us. Solid gold and nothing but. Hungry Mother be playing the hits, playing them hits, for you, jes' for youuuu . . .

(*Full-out manic now.*) Uh-huh! Into the smokey blue! Comin' at you! Get out de way! Hungry Mother gonna hammer, gonna glide, gonna slide, gonna bop, gonna drop, gonna dance dem ariel waves, til he get to you, yes you! Razzle you, dazzle you, blow you a-way! This one gonna hammer . . . gonna hammer you blue!

(*Dryly.*) Flatten you like a side of beef, sucker.

(*Mellifluous.*) This is WTWI, it's 7:34, the weather is *dark*, dormant species are stirring, cold and warm bloods both, muck is up, and I'm the Hungry Mother. The weather outlook is for continued existential dread under cloudy skies with scattered low-grade distress. Look out for the Greenhouse Effect . . . We'll be back, but first — a word about succulents —

(*Beat. Flicks switches.*) We're coming to you live, from our syncopated phonebooth high above the floating bridge in violation of *several* natural laws, searching, strolling, and trolling, for the sweetest music this side of Heaven.

(*Beat. Then:*) Back at you! This is the Hungry Mother, just barely holding on, at WTWI, the cold-water station with the bird's-eye view, on this beautifully indeterminate morning, bringin' you monster after musical monster. Chuckin' 'em down the pike, humpin' 'em up and over the DMZ, in a never-ending effort to make a dent in that purple purple texture. And right now I've got what you've all been waiting for — Hungry Mother's HAMMER OF THE WEEK! And Mother's Hammer for this week, forty seven with a silver bullet — "Fiberglass Felony Shoes" — something slick — by Hoover *and* the Navajos.

(*Friendly.*) And, as always, behind every Mother's Hammer of the Week — there's a human being. And a human interest story. You're probably hip to this already, but I'm gonna lay it on you anyway. Hoover — is a full-blooded, red-blooded *Native American*. One of several in the annals of illustrated American Pop.

(*Slight pause.*) Hoover had a monster a few years back: "Fiberglass Rock" — just a giant on the Res. And elsewhere. That, *mais oui*, was before the tragic accident in which Hoover — ah, I don't know if this is public knowledge — but, o why not grovel in gore? (*Bopping.*) With the fallout from his titanium monster, "Fiberglass Rock", Hoover put something down on a preowned dream, a Pontiac Superchief, drive it *away*. A steal. A *machine*. Four on the floor and three on the tree, a herd of horses under the hood! (*Beat. Solemn.*) Four flats. Cracked axle. Hoover — his heart as big and red as the great outdoors — goes down . . . with a wrench. The Superchief slips the jack—and pins Hoover by his . . . pickin' hand.

(*Beat.*) WIPE OUT!

(*Beat.*) Crushed dem bones to milk.

(*Rising frenzy.*) But now he's back. Back where he belongs! With the aid of a prosthetic device! Back on the charts again! PIONEER OF PATHO-ROCK! (*Slight pause. Then: warm, hip.*) Many happy returns of the day, Hoover, for you and yours.

(*Flicks switches. Mellow.*) The sun is up, *officially,* and all good things, according to the laws of thermodynamics, must come to an end. Join us—tomorrow—for something approaching solitude. WTWI now relents and gives up the ghost of its broadcasting day.

(*He flicks switches. The blue light, the Broadcast Indicator, goes 'off'. Over the loudspeakers, a woman's voice, live.*)

LOUD SPEAKER: Aspects of the Hungry Mother.

HUNGRY MOTHER: (*Reading from a book of matches.*) Success without college. Train at home. Do not mail matches.

LOUD SPEAKER: Hungry Mother hits the streets.

HUNGRY MOTHER: (*To* LOUD SPEAKER.) I be gone . . . but I lef' my name to carry on.

(HUNGRY MOTHER *shuffles into the street.* FREE LANCE *approaches. They recognize one another, tense, draw closer. They do a street dance, slow, sexy, dangerous. Freeze. They release.* FREE LANCE *slides back and out.*)

LOUD SPEAKER: Hungry Mother after hours.

(HUNGRY MOTHER *slides into the bar where there is a solitary figure drinking.*)

HUNGRY MOTHER: Belly Up.

BELLY UP: Say what?

HUNGRY MOTHER: Belly Up, it's been a coon's age.

BELLY UP: I know you?

HUNGRY MOTHER: Think it over.

BELLY UP: Buy me a drink.

HUNGRY MOTHER: City jail.

BELLY UP: Hungry Mother. What it is, Mom, what it is. How's it goin', Home? How goes the suppurating sore?

HUNGRY MOTHER: It's coming along. Thank you.

BELLY UP: Hungry Mother. Whose tones are legion. Hungry Mother, voice of darkness. Impressario of derangement. Tireless promoter of patho-rock. The man who'll air that wax despair.

HUNGRY MOTHER: When no one else will dare.

BELLY UP: The quintessential Cassandra. The damn Jonah who hacked his way out of the whale. Hungry Mother, the bleating gurgle of those who've had their throats cut.

HUNGRY MOTHER: You give me too much, Belly Up, my boy. It's all air time. Air-waves access, that's what it's all about. I just prop 'em up over the mike and let 'em bleed — gurgle gurgle pop short.

BELLY UP: Credit where credit is due.

HUNGRY MOTHER: Why, thank you, Brother Belly. It's a comfort to know that, a genuine solid comfort. My cup is filled with joy to know that someone's *really* listening. Why, late at night and on into the dawn, I have my doubts, I surely do. Casting my pearls — over the brink —

BELLY UP: (*Picking it up.*) Into the trough. On a wing and a prayer. Before the swine of despond. (*Pause.*) Not so, Hungry Mother, not so; not a bit. Your words hang on the barbed wire of evening, glistering in the urban nether vapors like a diamond choke chain on black satin.

HUNGRY MOTHER: Belly Up, you have the gift, you surely do. It's a wonder you don't pursue some purely *metaphorical* calling.

BELLY UP: My sentiments precisely. Please indulge me as I continue to flesh out my figure . . . Hungry Mother turns tricks quicker than a dockside hooker hustling her habit. He fences insights, pawns epiphanies. And we redeem those tickets in nasty corners. You the laser wizard. The magnetic pulse. The cardiac arrest. The barbarians have smashed the plate glass window of Western Civ and are running amok in the bargain basement. (HUNGRY MOTHER *applauds*.) Thank you. Transistor insights. Diode data. Crystal-tube revelations. That why we dial you in, Mothah.

HUNGRY MOTHER: You and who else?

BELLY UP: You'd be surprised. (*Pause*.) I got a chopper on the roof.

HUNGRY MOTHER: What?

BELLY UP: (*Winks and laughs*.) I got a chopper on the roof.

HUNGRY MOTHER: (*Beat*) Look, I got a question for you. Say the hoodlums, punks, pervos, perps, feral children, coupon clippers, and all the other bargain basement thrift shoppers, say they skip Housewares. Sporting goods. Electronic lingerie. Junior misses. All the lower floor diversions. And go straight for the suites at the top.

BELLY UP: (*Laughs*.) I got a chopper on the roof! Got my own sweet chopper to take me outa this! See? I anticipate your question. Like I anticipate the situation. And the answer. An-ti-cipate. Got to have that getaway hatch, Mother. Got to have it. Even a fool can see what's comin'. (*Slight pause*.) You're *sensitive*, Mother. We can read you like a rectal therm. Any little fluctuation. Fuck Dow Jones. We got the good stuff. (*Slight pause*.) We tune you in, we know when to split. Any little fluc. You our miner's canary, Mother. We hang you out there on the hook and hope you smell the gas in time. You croak—we go.

HUNGRY MOTHER: I'll try to give you five.

BELLY UP: Man, five is all I ask. My ears are glued.

HUNGRY MOTHER: Keep those cards and letters coming. So I know you're still glued.

BELLY UP: Don't sweat. As long as you still singing, we still listening. When you on the air, we say "Hosannah!"

HUNGRY MOTHER: Say "Hungry!", sweetheart.

(*They toast. Darkness. As* HUNGRY MOTHER *walks back into the studio his amplified voice booms over the PA.*)

HUNGRY MOTHER: (*On tape.*) Hoover is crawling back from near annihilation, a mighty mean accident for the little red man —

(*Sound of car crash.*)

(*Lights.* HUNGRY MOTHER *freezes at the mike.*)

LOUD SPEAKER: Further aspects of the Hungry Mother — *revealed!* For the very first time — the Hungry Mother in jail!

(*The jail appears in a flash of light:* CHARLIE SAMOA *and* JOHNNY *and* JIMMY. *They babble in several languages, cursing. Jail vanishes. Lights up on* HUNGRY MOTHER. *He breaks freeze. Flicks switches, blue light "on".*)

HUNGRY MOTHER: (*High speed.*) Career-wise, a mighty mean accident, a tough break for the little red man. We'll be back with the Prick Hit of the Week — ha, ha, oh — Freudian faux pas — Pick Hit of the Week, "Nuking the Chinks", by Dragon Lady and the Flying Paper Tigers, but first — a word about peccaries . . . Friends — like so many vanishing species, these ugly little critters need your help. A tusk or two, a hoof, a stewpot of glue. It's all over for them, but what about their by-products? (*Dramatic*) Next week — blue whales and dog food.

(*Mellifluous.*) This is WTWI, the station with no visible means of support, this is a weekday, this is the Hungry Mother, blistering the dusk to dawn shift, grinding 'em down and pulling 'em out, monster after effervescent monster. Holocaust warnings are up. They continue to machine-gun survivors outside our studio. And the ozone keeps oozing away! And now — Mother's got what you've all been waiting for — nearly an hour of unrelieved agony! Twilight Desperation News! Brought to you by Universal Antipathy — Universal Antipathy, engendering tensions all over the globe — and by Sorghum — a fast food whose time is ripe ripe ripe! Invest in sorghum futures today! And now the hour's top headlines.

(Newscaster tones, pounding out a teletype rhythm on a tiny plastic typewriter as he speaks.)

"Killer Bees from Brazil Drop Texas Rangers in Their Tracks" . . . "Starfish Finish Off Great Barrier Reef" . . . quote, "The sky's the limit", endquote . . . Couple Flees Talking Bear. . . . One last note for you nature lovers: fossil fuels now coat 87% of the known universe. Those slicks are tough. No wonder dry-cleaning costs an arm and two legs . . . On the international beat, expatriate citizens of the island of Malta are demanding restitution from the community of nations. Malta was mugged early yesterday by two large black countries with hydrogen knuckles . . . it sank without a trace. Shades of Krakatoa. The usual measures to contain the radioactive dusk are being implemented with, as one official so succinctly put it, little or no chance of success. We'll have more this hour on the latest in genetic mutation, both here and abroad but first — late, and leg, breaking sports . . .

(HUNGRY MOTHER picks up a pair of mechanical birds, and winds them into motion: they waddle and squawk.)

HUNGRY MOTHER: *(To the birds.)* You're brilliant and you're blue . . . conjugal bijou babies. Doves of love. Beaks of lazuli, warbles of tin. *(The birds wind down and halt.)*

HUNGRY MOTHER: *(Intones.)* Wound down.

(He eats beans from a can.)

HUNGRY MOTHER: Interlude In Which Beans Are Eaten.

LOUD SPEAKER: The authorized autobiography of the Hunry Mother. The truth — with a twist!

HUNGRY MOTHER: First . . . lemme say . . . unequivocally — and between bites — that the Hungry Mother was made,

not born. Not of woman born. Heh heh heh. Puts me up
there with the all-time greats, right? I want to be most em-
phatic about this. The Hungry Mother is—my own crea-
tion. Nom de wireless! Home-made man! So fine!

LOUD SPEAKER: Hungry scat! Mother doo wop! Fonky
Mothah! (*Loudspeaker*)

HUNGRY MOTHER: (*To the mike, sings*)

>Put on your felony shoes
>Put on your felony shoes
>Everybody gonna want you to
>Put on your felony shoes
>Come on wit' me
>We gonna cut somethin' loose
>We gonna boost
>Something fine
>And shiny and new
>If you'll jes'
>Put on your felony shoes

LOUD SPEAKER: And now—number one with a dum-dum
—Mother's Hammer Too Hot To Handle!

HUNGRY MOTHER: And now, getting tons of extended hot
air play in S and M loading zones and up and down the
leather docks from coast to disco coast—the newest from
Hoover and the Navajos—parvenu of patho-rock—"Fiberglass Creep and the Rotating Tumors!"

(*He begins teletype noise, and speaks gravely.*) Police today busted
a waterfront distillery, arresting twenty-seven adults. The
distillery produces a wine brewed from the sores of children,
which is quite popular locally and in the contiguous states,
and easily available without a prescription. The cops said
the kids were kept in cages underneath the piers because,
quote, the salt water facilitates the festeration process, endquote. The perpetrators will be arraigned tomorrow on tax-
evasion charges, and the children, several hundred of them,
have been released into the custody of leading lending institutions . . .

(*Upbeat.*) The block buster scoop this solid gold weekend—
thousands of citizens roaming the streets in states of bliss-out

and fat poisoning. Watch out for those psychoparalytic hallucinations. They can be tricky. Speaking of weather, the outlook through the weekend remains bleak. Our five-day forecast calls for continued historical uneasiness mingled with intermittent bouts of apocalyptic epiphany, and occasional oxygen debt—under cloudy skies. So wear your rubbers . . .

(*Jaunty*.) This has been The Agony News Hour, an exclusive twilight feature of WTWI, with your host, the Hungry Mother. Stay tuned for "Name My Race", the game guaranteed to offend nearly everyone, brought to you by Ethnic Considerations, dedicated to exacerbating racial tensions through violence—Ethnic Considerations, a hallmark of the Twentieth Century, don't leave home without them. And now it's time once again for *Dear Mother*.

(*He holds a stack of letters impaled on a bowie knife. He plucks off the top letter and reads it in a cheery DJ voice.*)

HUNGRY MOTHER: "Dear Mother: My boyfriend has a fishhook in the end of his penis. This makes congress difficult. Even painful. What can I do about it? Signed, Afraid to Swallow." (*He crumples it up and tosses it away.*)

HUNGRY MOTHER: Eighty-six that. Prick Hit of the Week. Cranks. Who do they think they're kidding. I'm not just fooling around here. (*Next letter.*)

"Dear Mother: My husband is an unreconstructed Stalinist. He refuses to de-Stalinize, knowing that recantation would expose him as an accomplice to the most heinous crimes of this vile century. This ideological rift has been the recrudescent cause of numerous domestic conflicts and, I believe, threatens the dialectic of our marriage. Just yesterday I suggested opening bilateral summit talks on the question of rehabilitating Trotsky for the family shrine of revolutionary heroes, and he broke my jaw. Dear Mother, for the sake of the children, what do you suggest? Signed, Just a Bourgeois Social Fascist At Heart."

(*Slight pause.*) Dear Just a Bourgeois: I suggest a fight to the death with needle-nosed pliers. (*He tears it up.*) What's happening to the language? It's scary, Jim. The Great Nuance Crisis is upon us. One last letter for this fiscal year.

(*A cheery DJ voice.*) "Dear Mother: I listen to you every night. You are a great comfort to me. I don't know what I'd do without you. Please help me, Mother. It hurts so bad I can barely talk. Signed, Despe te." (*Slight pause.*) Dear Desperate . . . For once I'm at a loss for words. (*Slight pause.*) Perhaps you've mistaken me for you natural mother. I'm nobody's mama, sweetheart. (*Slight pause.*) Dear Desperate, I can't help you — if you don't give me something more to go on. Who are you, where, and what's troubling you, Bunky. Please try and nail it down a little closer, dear . . . Friends, got an *esoteric* problem? Send it to Mother and he'll devour it for you. And now it's time once again for — *The Big Dose, A Taste Of Things To Come,* when the Mother lets you in on what it's really gonna be like once the rude boys start playing for keeps. So here it is, tonight, at no extra charge, Hungry Mother brings you more than two hours of — dead air. Enjoy.

(*Flicks switches. Blue light "off". Shrugs into an overcoat and goes into the street. Encounters* FREE LANCE. *They do their dance, as before. Freeze. Slight pause.*)

LOUD SPEAKER: Hungry Mother — Street Solo!

(*He runs downstage scatting some "theme" music. At the appropriate moment:*)

LOUD SPEAKER: And now! Heeeeeeeere's . . . HUNGRY!!

HUNGRY MOTHER: (*Bopping.*) Could be Japanese! . . . Genetic . . . engineering! Charnel — numbah — five! *Smoke!* (*Changing gears.*) Friends . . . let's have a chat. Heart to heart. Would Mother hand you a bum steer? . . . As you know, the suggested agenda topic for today's luncheon is . . . Why Do De Gu'mint Be De Boz Ob De Scag Trade, or . . . Methadone — Magic or Madness? . . . But I, uh, I have something of more immediate import to . . . impart. (*Slight pause.*) Friends . . . let's talk about . . . *crude drugs.*

(*Clears throat.*) Brothers and sisters, I was down at the Hotel Abyss the other day, down at that old Hotel Abyss, when I chance to run into an old old friend of mine. A legend in his

own time. A man who knows the score. Who never lets the
sun get in his eyes. A man with no holes in his cosmic glove
. . . I am speakin' of course about . . . Cocaine Ricky.
(*Slight pause.*) Your friend and mine. (*Slight pause.*) Brothers
and sisters, Cocaine Ricky tell me there be some mighty cold
stuff goin' 'round out there, and I just want you to watch it.
Very very cold. Ice cold. Dude be pushin', be pushin' it as
snow. You know? Snow fall. Snow job. Snow blind. Snow
go. (*Slight pause.*) Ain't snow. It's *Lance*. Lance. (*Slight pause.*)
Instant death. (*Slight pause.*) Powdered nerve gas. (*Slight
pause.*) Government issue. Sooo cooold. Huh!

(HUNGRY MOTHER *and* FREE LANCE *enter the studio. She is
dressed to street-kill.*)

FREE LANCE: This place look like a Cargo Cult beach head.
You always had a knack for dives, Mother.

HUNGRY MOTHER: Thank you very much.

FREE LANCE: I don't truck with the radio much. It doesn't
occur to me. It's not one of my . . . habits. I don't have time
for media. What I'm saying is — I haven't caught your show.

HUNGRY MOTHER: Fuck you very much.

FREE LANCE: Don't be bitter.

HUNGRY MOTHER: Where you live dese days, honey chile?

FREE LANCE: On the docks.

HUNGRY MOTHER: Couldn't cotch me down dere, anyways.

FREE LANCE: Armegeddon Arms. Condos de rigueur. Sing
Sing singles. Know them?

HUNGRY MOTHER: No, but I know the neighborhood. In-
timately. Whatchew dew down dere, woman? You ain't involved with dem child distellers, is you?

FREE LANCE: I don't believe so. Not to my knowledge. It
hasn't come to my attention. You ought to come visit me,
Mother.

HUNGRY MOTHER: I should, it's true.

FREE LANCE: It's much nicer than this, really. Chrome furniture. It'd be a change.

HUNGRY MOTHER: I don't get out much. Don't leave the 'hood. I'm cooped.

FREE LANCE: Cooped.

HUNGRY MOTHER: Up.

FREE LANCE: It's very outre, you know. Swank and chic in the nastier neighborhoods. I just crave the danger. It's narcotic. And there's really nothing to worry about. The building itself is just the best. Impregnable. White boys from Missoura.

HUNGRY MOTHER: I can appreciate that.

FREE LANCE: Eliminates the Fifth Column spectre. My parents *never* hired black servants. No mammies for me. Don't tell me about race loyalty. When push comes to shove, I mean. Save on silver, too. And being near the water gives me a warm warm feeling.

HUNGRY MOTHER: For a quick and hasty exit.

FREE LANCE: When the time comes. We've made the arrangements. There won't be any trouble. When the time comes.

HUNGRY MOTHER: You'll take some casualties, of course.

FREE LANCE: When the time comes. Probably. Of course. One learns to live with one's losses.

HUNGRY MOTHER: Don't one? That reminds me. (*He flicks switches: blue light "on".*)

HUNGRY MOTHER: (*Red hot.*) Back at you, sports, this is *the* Hungry Momma, the one and only, the original Hungry Momma, accept no substitutes, coming at you out of the blue-black on this elusive weekday ay-em in a possibly transitional stage in the floodtide of human affairs. Let the historians decide. You've been listening—to more than two

hours of—*dead air*. C'est frommage. The time just got away
from me there, mon cher. We'll be phasing out our broadcasting day with vanishing species animal noises, what a
hoot. And we'll finish off with a new one, got it in the mail
today, from the purveyors of patho-rock, Hoover and the
Navajos, their latest—"Fiberglass Repairman"! (*Sings a
slow blues, keeping the beat with handslams.*)

HUNGRY MOTHER: (*Sings.*)

> I'll insulate yo' home
> I'll fibreglass yo' phone
> An' I'll Navajogate
> The little woman
> Befo' yo'
> Back is turned.

(*Low key.*) Just breaks my goddamn heart. Sayonara, kids.
I'll be back later in the week at my regularly unscheduled
time. So—keep dialing and keep *hoping*. This is the Hungry
Mother, the man who put the *hun* back in hungry, remind-
ing you to stay cool, take it light, and say—*Hungry!* (*Slight
pause, then cool and bureaucratic.*) WTWI has now pissed
away/Its broadcasting day. (HUNGRY MOTHER *switches the
blue light "off".*)

FREE LANCE: I'm surprised you don't lose your license.

HUNGRY MOTHER: Tell you the secret of my success.
Nobody hears me. This tube gear eats it. Raw. I got a radius
range of under a mile. Barely covers one police precinct. I'm
very proud of my precinct. It ain't much, but it's home. I
pledge allegiance to my precinct . . . Nobody lives up here.
'S all bomb-outs. Gutted projects. Arsonated rubble.

FREE LANCE: Listener response?

HUNGRY MOTHER: Rubble don't write a lot of post cards.
The junkies call me sometimes. *Hit* Line requests. Sugar
Bear and Oz. They call on their anniversary. Four years, a
mutual monkey. Many happy returns of the day. Born to
junk. Scrapin' along and strung far-out on meth-a-done.
Sugar Bear and Oz, this is the hit, this is the one, to which

you first shot each other up and fell in love, oh so long ago. Sugar Bear and Oz, up on the roof, this one's for you. So slick.

FREE LANCE: (*Laughs.*) One hears stories.

HUNGRY MOTHER: It's been known to happen.

FREE LANCE: About you, dear. One hears them. In the air. Snatches. All over. Faceless celeb. You ought to take precautions. You have more listeners than you think. Than you might imagine.

HUNGRY MOTHER: Funny you should say that. I have been getting more letters. Got one today, it was a mistake. She mistook me. It's a serious letter.

FREE LANCE: Aren't they all?

HUNGRY MOTHER: Just crazy. This one was crazy, too. But serious.

FREE LANCE: What are you going to do about it?

HUNGRY MOTHER: What can you do about it?

FREE LANCE: Respond.

(*Pause.*)

HUNGRY MOTHER: She wants help.

FREE LANCE: Then help her.

HUNGRY MOTHER: How?

(*Pause*)

FREE LANCE: I've changed my name.

HUNGRY MOTHER: Ah.

FREE LANCE: I've *altered* it.

HUNGRY MOTHER: I remember. You were into brand names. Rumor had it.

FREE LANCE: Generic. Not brand, generic.

HUNGRY MOTHER: "Polish Vodka".

FREE LANCE: Very tasty. I was all over the society pages. But I gave it up when I left the Agency. It's Free Lance now.

HUNGRY MOTHER: Oooo. Evocative. (*Slight pause.*) I prefer Polish Vodka.

(*Pause.*)

FREE LANCE: If wishes were horses.

(*Pause.*)

HUNGRY MOTHER: If the river was whiskey.

(*Pause.*)

FREE LANCE: You've always been the Hungry Mother. Ever since I've known you. (*Pause.*) I work for the Mook now.

HUNGRY MOTHER: The Mook. Oh my.

FREE LANCE: Again. That's how I heard about you. That's how I tracked you down.

HUNGRY MOTHER: The Mook? Listens to me?

FREE LANCE: Faithfully.

HUNGRY MOTHER: It's almost an honor. In a patho-spastic sort of way.

FREE LANCE: He told me you were back on the air.

HUNGRY MOTHER: I'll have to upgrade my shit. Can't have no cut-rate shit if the Mook's tuned in.

FREE LANCE: You ought to be more careful. The Mook's worried about your license.

(*Slight pause.*)

HUNGRY MOTHER: I don't have no license. And I'd bet my momma he knows that. His momma, too. How's his reception? Where's he based?

FREE LANCE: He *floats*.

(*Pause.*)

HUNGRY MOTHER: Why'd you go back?

FREE LANCE: Oh, honey. (*Laughs.*) Oh honey. I'd drink his bathwater. (*Beat.*) I did super at the Agency. it was dull, darling. Dull as crushed rock. For them. On my own, it's a breeze. *Free Lance.* Don't you just dig the shit out of it? (*Pause. Cool smile; sardonic*) I *love* the way he beats me, Mother. Swell hands. Something of a setback for personal liberation, right Mother? (*Pause.*) I tried to cut him loose.

HUNGRY MOTHER: You sure you're not involved with those kids? Ask Mook.

FREE LANCE: Mook doesn't do kids. You're very tender, Mother, but I could never count on you. Maybe after the revolution.

HUNGRY MOTHER: Right. The coup d'etat will make us straight . . . Thanks for stopping by, uh, Free Lance. Always nice to see you.

FREE LANCE: You, too, Mother. Like old times. Good, yes?

HUNGRY MOTHER: Absolutely golden. Better than a poke in the eye with a sharp stick. The best of them.

FREE LANCE: Don't become a stranger, Mother. (*She drifts into the street.*)

(HUNGRY MOTHER *switches blue light 'on'.*)

HUNGRY MOTHER: And now a word from one of our sponsors. The Bantustan Shooting Gallery's One Hundred and Sixth Street Branch will be open twenty-four hours a day throughout the holiday weekend for your intravenous entertainment. They're stocking up on your favorite brands of smack, so get your shit together and get on over to One Hundred and Sixth Street now. They're running a special on Spearchucker, got a brand new batch of Black on Black, the ever-popular Pussy Whipped is always on hand, and, fresh off the boat, while it lasts, that perennial Bantustan favorite, White Flight. And the one thousandth customer this holiday weekend will receive, free of extenuating circumstances, a red-hot two-tone maroon Jew Canoe with fresh plates, plenty of mirror surface, and brand new Cuban credit card with sanitary nozzle. That's this weekend at the Bantustan One Hundred and Sixth Street Shooting Gallery — *rush* on over.

(*He turns the blue light off. Shrugs into his coat.*)

LOUD SPEAKER: A walk — on the wild side.

(HUNGRY MOTHER *hits the street, and slides into the bar.* BELLY UP *is drinking, alone. He's wearing his old sergeant's fatigue jacket, the shadow of the chevrons still visible on the sleeve.*)

BELLY UP: You're taking off like a target-seeking, heat-sensitive, laser-directed, anti-personnel device. Stuffed with shrapnel. *Plastic* shrapnel. (*Laughs.*) Cluster bomb, Mom. Cluster bomb! (*Slight pause.*) Plastic shrap don't X-ray. That's the holy beauty of it. X-rays can't cope. Can't lo-cate it. Can't dig it out. (*Slight pause.*) Cluster *fuck.* (*Slight pause.*) Hungry Mother, the voice of the voiceless, the articulator of the ineffable, the thing that goes bump in the night. I never miss a show.

HUNGRY MOTHER: I wish I could say the same.

BELLY UP: You're getting better. More conscientious. Know what I saw? In a window? A record. By Hoover and the Navajos.

(*Long pause.*)

HUNGRY MOTHER: Outstanding. (*Pause.*) Was there a picture? What'd they look like?

BELLY UP: No picture. Crazy thing. It came in a fiberglass dust jacket. I got that shit up my ass. It burns like hell. Gets into every nook and cranny. Fibers. They're far out. They're a far-out group. Insulation. Navajogation. Kills me. This — ?

HUNGRY MOTHER: Patho-rock.

BELLY UP: Knocks my socks off. I love it. Better than mime for the blind. Heaps better. "Fiberglass Finger Fuck"! "Fiberglass Felony Shoes"! "Carcinogenic Concierge"! Can you dig it? Blows me away. You ought to have them on the show.

HUNGRY MOTHER: Don't bug me, Belly Up. I just get this stuff in the mail.

BELLY UP: From the record company.

HUNGRY MOTHER: From *nobody.* It just floats in on the tide.

BELLY UP: You're gonna break 'em, Mother. You're gonna break 'em big. When I saw them in a store I was *fiberglassted.*

Heh heh. I had no idea they were for real. I thought you . . . *created* them, you know? The holy power of PR.

HUNGRY MOTHER: So did I. In a way, I mean. As far as I know, I don't know if there really is a "Hoover and."

BELLY UP: I purchased it.

HUNGRY MOTHER: LP or single?

BELLY UP: LP. A botanica. Voodoo boutique. Haitian herb shop. I was on the prowl for a pack of mojo and a slice of John the Conqueroo. Saw it in amongst the loas and the gris-gris.

HUNGRY MOTHER: That's a good sign. That's encouraging. Those places are more underground than I am. Maybe we can nip this in the bud. I'd hate for it to get out of hand. I never intended to inflict Hoover and the Navajos on the general public. Something like this. A trend.

BELLY UP: Maybe they're ready for it. Look at it this way — Hungry Mother, hit maker!

HUNGRY MOTHER: Right. Just another top-forty jock. Sounds good. I want it. I need it. I want to have impact . . . I'm a fucking artist, man. I want to be taken seriously.

BELLY UP: To which end?

HUNGRY MOTHER: The bitter end, natch. Tell me, Belly, to what do you attribute my sudden surge of popularity?

BELLY UP: To the fact you're coming in loud and clear. Everywhere I go, Hungry Mother, that's who folks be talkin' bout.

HUNGRY MOTHER: Where do you go?

BELLY UP: Dark places. Places that slide. Places that glide. Places that aren't quite solid underfoot. You're becoming very big on the fringes. Amongst the rubble. Don't be downcast. You're articulating a definite need.

HUNGRY MOTHER: Don't think I'm not grateful. I like it. I love it. Here I thought I was only reaching my local rubble, and now you tell me I'm a smash in the rubble all over town.

BELLY UP: An idea whose time has come.

HUNGRY MOTHER: It's a heavy responsibility. Walk me home, Belly Up.

BELLY UP: Sorry. Not at this hour. I don't leave the bar.

HUNGRY MOTHER: What are you afraid of?

(*Pause.*)

BELLY UP: Get your hungry ass over here on time, I'll give you a lift. (*Beat*) Back to the World.

HUNGRY MOTHER: I hear you. (*Beat.*) I hear you (*Beat.*) Belly Up, I keep getting these letters.

(*The bar fades.* HUNGRY MOTHER *on the streets.*)

LOUD SPEAKER: Aspects of the Hungry Mother. The Hungry Mother in Jail.

(*The jail scene appears:* CHARLIE SAMOA, *and* JOHNNIE *and* JIMMY *in silhouette, cursing in polyglot.*)

HUNGRY MOTHER: This is a flashback. A reprise. I don't think I care for this right now.

LOUD SPEAKER: Mañana, mañana. You're just postponing the inevitable. It's on the playlist, baby. This is a very *tight* playlist.

HUNGRY MOTHER: Maybe later. How about? I want a reprieve from this reprise.

LOUD SPEAKER: (*Miffed.*) You're just postponing the sooner or later, babe.

HUNGRY MOTHER: Fuck off.

(*Jail fades.* HUNGRY MOTHER *runs into the studio. He flicks the blue light "on".*)

HUNGRY MOTHER: Dead air redux! Those acid flashbacks are murder! Hey! This be your happy, hopping, and high-speed Hungry Mother — doin' it to you before you can do it to yourself. Our special this hour, Hungry Mother's Horoscope — a penetrating peek at the Big Zee. So stick around and watch the Mother scope it and dope it — just for you. Also on the bill this o-bliterated amorphous morn — broken glass . . . and — Hungry Mother's Consumer Guide to Junk, where to score and what to pay, where to shoot and what to say, all the places and all the pushers, why not have the best possible habit in this, the Best, of all possible worlds? But first — this hour's top headlines.

(*Teletype sound and newscaster voice.*) That illegal cordial made from kid pus is still circulating. Several deaths have been reported . . . More mastodon sightings in the North Cascades . . . Wolves in the outlying districts — if you're walking in the suburbs this morning, *remember* — Wolf Warnings are up. Pedestrians are advised to travel in packs and exercise the usual precautions . . . We'll be back after something brief. This is WTWI, and this is the Hungry Mother, live — if you call this living, from our Twilight Studios. Remember to say, "Hungry!" And now, another interminable episode of "Sexual Shadow Land," the show that's sweeping the station.

(*Rod Serling*:) His was an ordinary fetish — with a difference — (*Phone rings.*) I'll get it. (*Flicks switches.*) You're on the air! Hey there!

JANIS: (*Live, over P.A.*) Hello? (*Hello? hello?*)

HUNGRY MOTHER: Turn down your radio! Please! Turn it down!

JANIS: What? (*What? what?*)

HUNGRY MOTHER: Turn that radio down! Turn it down! You're on the air! Trust me!

JANIS: Okay! (*Okay! okay!*)

(*When* JANIS *next speaks, the echo and feedback are gone.*)

JANIS: Better?

HUNGRY MOTHER: Much! I'd starve on feedback. What can Mother do for you? What can you do for Mother?

JANIS: Oh, Mother, I know. I listen to you all the time. I sit by the radio. I wait. I don't want to miss you. I hardly go out anymore. I don't.

HUNGRY MOTHER: You sound like a fan.

JANIS: Believe me, I am . . . I am. I don't go out anyway. But —I am. A fan. It's a comfort.

(*Pause.*)

HUNGRY MOTHER: Yes? Was there something else? You're killing my air.

JANIS: My name is Janis, Mother. I'd like to see you. You don't know me. I'm a stranger. We've never met.

HUNGRY MOTHER: Sure. C'mon up.

(*Slight pause.*)

JANIS: This is serious. I want to meet you. (*Slight pause.*) Mother. I really need to see you. Please . . . Can you tell me how to get there?

HUNGRY MOTHER: Sure. Ah, it's One Marauder Avenue, just past Faghag Park. Always hungry to have visitors in the studio, little lady.

(*He hangs up. Looks pointedly at the "on" blue light.*)

HUNGRY MOTHER: Whatever happens. Hang loose. Go with the flow. Lean with the scene. Strive with the jive. Fuck it.

(*The Jail scene appears.* HUNGRY MOTHER *walks into it. The trio regards him ravenously.*)

CHARLIE SAMOA: My name is Charlie Samoa.

HUNGRY MOTHER: Right away.

CHARLIE SAMOA: And these are . . . the Samoans. (*Indicating the transvestites.*) Johnnie Sucrose — take a bow, sweetie — and Jimmy Shillelagh.

HUNGRY MOTHER: Charmed, I'm sure. My name is . . . uh, professionaly I'm known as, uh, a.k.a. —

CHARLIE SAMOA: We know who you are —

JOHNNIE SUCROSE: There's no need to shit us —

JIMMY SHILLELAGH: We never miss a show —

JOHNNIE SUCROSE: We'd know the golden tones anywhere. We're big big fans of yours.

CHARLIE SAMOA: But we got a question. The question is — what are you doing here?

JOHNNIE SUCROSE: Not that we mind, you understand —

JIMMY SHILLELAGH: Not that we're not thrilled —

CHARLIE SAMOA: Even honored —

JOHNNIE SUCROSE: But it comes as something of a shock —

JIMMY SHILLELAGH: To say the least.

CHARLIE SAMOA: We hope it does not have to do with your superb radio show —

JOHNNIE SUCROSE: Of which we never miss a single segment —

JIMMY SHILLELAGH: At considerable risk to ourselves in view of the multiple restrictions pertaining to the use of, access to, and ownership of tube gear and ghetto blasters in this, ah, ah —

JOHNNIE SUCROSE: *Penal* institution.

CHARLIE and JIMMY: Yeah.

HUNGRY MOTHER: You guys are desatively bonnaroo. A matched set. Siamese triplets, joined at the mouth. I predict a great future for you, should you consider it. Give me a call when you get out.

(*Pause.*)

CHARLIE SAMOA: Answer the question.

JOHNNIE SUCROSE: It behooves me.

JIMMY SHILLELAGH: Believe me.

CHARLIE SAMOA: Believe him.

(*Pause.*)

HUNGRY MOTHER: Criminal mischief . . . I . . . mmm . . . I shattered a subway window. (*Slight pause.*) With a golfclub.

(*Pause.*)

CHARLIE SAMOA: *Why?*

HUNGRY MOTHER: I was . . . *sore.*

(*Pause.*)

JOHNNIE SUCROSE: How many strokes?

HUNGRY MOTHER: Just one. (*Slight pause.*) Nine iron.

JIMMY SHILLELAGH: Good choice.

(*Pause.*)

CHARLIE SAMOA: Penny ante, Mother, strictly penny ante.

JOHNNIE SUCROSE: We are very disappoint.

JIMMY SHILLELAGH: Although at the same time greatly relieved that this does not have to do with your illegal yet highly entertaining radio program.

HUNGRY MOTHER: Oh, no. Not on your sweet. It's not illegal, anyway. *Para*-legal. I've never had any trouble. Nobody listens.

CHARLIE SAMOA: We do.

JOHNNIE SUCROSE: We're interested —

JIMMY SHILLELAGH: We're concerned —

CHARLIE SAMOA: We're anxiety ridden.

JOHNNIE SUCROSE: You don't have a license.

HUNGRY MOTHER: What a bitch. They license every goddamn thing in this goddamn city. You need a license to change a light bulb and a permit to take a piss.

CHARLIE SAMOA: Good thing, too. Where would we be without social order? You got to maintain it.

JOHNNIE SUCROSE: Very impor-*tant*.

JIMMY SHILLELAGH: Somebody's got to do it. Gotta have that social scheme.

CHARLIE SAMOA: A modicum of status quo.

JIMMY SHILLELAGH: To go along with a lot of expensive tube gear and no visible means of support.

JOHNNIE SUCROSE: And no license.

HUNGRY MOTHER: Very acute. Ah . . . where do you get your dope on me?

CHARLIE SAMOA: We asked around.

JIMMY SHILLELAGH: We checked the score.

JOHNNIE SUCROSE: We heard it through the grapevine.

(*The* SAMOANS *laugh raucously, then subside.*)

HUNGRY MOTHER: And that's how you come to be such . . . fans.

CHARLIE SAMOA: Thereby hangs a tale. It begins with a grudge. As most tales do. I was freelancin'. That's my thing. A little liaison. A middle-man shuffle 'tween U.S. Guv Intelligence cats and a certain Kuomingtang warlord. Local scag baron . . . Am I boring you? Got a minute?

HUNGRY MOTHER: Not at all. I mean certainly, yes, most certainly, I do.

CHARLIE SAMOA: Where am I?

JOHNNIE SUCROSE: (*Suggestively.*) The Golden Triangle.

JIMMY SHILLELAGH: Enmeshed in webs. High intrigue.

JOHNNIE SUCROSE: Boo-coo bucks.

JIMMY SHILLELAGH: So fine.

JOHNNIE SUCROSE: *Sweet.*

CHARLIE SAMOA: Put a lid on it. Oh by the way, Mother, your junk reports are . . . very helpful — somewhat fanciful — but very informational in a metaphorical sort of way. We're grateful, Mother. Say thank you, boys and girls.

JOHNNIE and JIMMY: Thank you, Mother.

(*Long pause.*)

HUNGRY MOTHER: You're not supposed to take that . . . (*Pause.*) Sure. Sure.

CHARLIE SAMOA: We think you got your finger on something. Some sort of . . . *pulse.* But I digress. (*Sniffs.*) In the course of negotiating these delicate, er, negotiations, I happened to run into certain disagreements with, that is to say, run afoul of an associate more of a colleague actually, concerning in connection with distribution rights . . . very complex. This gentleman . . . in order to press me, in order to,

I suppose, exert a primitive kind of leverage — kidnapped my daughter. (*Pause.*) When this rather crude ploy failed to have the desired effect, he did something very unpleasant to her. (*Pause.*) Nobody pushes me around. I want you to understand, Mother, that she'll be all right. I'm convinced of that. My daughter means everything to me. You know that, don't you Mother? *Her* mother was a *slut*, but she means everything to me. (*Pause.*) I went to his apartment house. I walk past the doorman. He didn't even see me. I'm a ghost. I walk up the back stair. Two at a time. No hurry, I was in no hurry. I rang the bell. Bang bang. I put the muzzle up, the muzzle of my magnum up — against the eyehole, the glass peephole. I rang the bell. He came to the door, I could hear his footsteps. He slid the cover back. Fffffffffttt. The cover of the peephole back. Click. Who could this be? His stomach's falling out. He couldn't see nothing, you understand. To him it just looked dark. But it was *steel*. (*Slight pause.*) He put his eye up to the glass. I make a clicking sound in the back of my throat. Click. Click. I shot him through the eye. Through the glass. That's how it was. I blew his fucking head apart.

(*Pause.*)

HUNGRY MOTHER: Why are they in here?

CHARLIE SAMOA: Ask 'em

HUNGRY MOTHER: Her. How can she be here?

JOHNNIE SUCROSE: I'm his conjugular visitor.

(*Slight pause. They laugh.*)

CHARLIE SAMOA: Pull the strings, Mom, you got to pull the strings.

(*They are laughing, shouting, pushing and shoving* HUNGRY MOTHER — *a mock mugging. At last,* HUNGRY MOTHER *breaks away. A moment, then:*)

HUNGRY MOTHER: I have to be going now.

CHARLIE SAMOA: Take it light —

JOHNNIE SUCROSE: Everything'll be all right—

JIMMY SHILLELAGH: Uptight and out of sight!

(*They are laughing again.*)

JOHNNIE SUCROSE: Out of state! Out of state!

CHARLIE SAMOA: That's good! Out of state! Johnnie, you kill me, babe!

JOHNNIE SUCROSE: Don't become a stranger!

JIMMY SHILLELAGH: Right!Right!Right!

(*Raucous laughter. They fade.* HUNGRY MOTHER *walks out and into the studio, up to the mike; blue light is still "on".*)

HUNGRY MOTHER: And while we're waiting for our mystery girl guest, here's Hungry Mother's Horo-scope. (*Mellifluous, honeyed.*) Virgo: your stars are black dwarves, be advised. But don't take it too hard, my dear. Thermodynamic entropy comes to us all. Libra: proceed with caution. A romantic entanglement may lead to a social disease. Sagittarius: your moon is in eclipse and your spouse in the house of your best friend. Taurus: your moon is in Uranus. Success is light-years away. Capricorn: copasetic! Aries: if you open your mouth, I wanna see some teeth. Leo: you were so ugly when you were born, the doctor slapped your mother. Gemini: once black, they never come back. Cancer: you've got it, what can I say? Tough nuggies. Moloch: take the first-born boy-child of every house—(*Phone rings.*)

Hang on! The lines are burning up! (*Switch flicking.*) Hello? Maybe I'll turn this mother into a *talk* show! Hello! You're *radio*-active!

THE MOOK: (*Live, over P.A.*) The planets are propitious. Hello, Mother.

HUNGRY MOTHER: Hey.

THE MOOK: How's by you?

HUNGRY MOTHER: Passable.

THE MOOK: Long time no you know.

HUNGRY MOTHER: Not long enough. You know?

THE MOOK: I'm looking for Free Lance.

(*Slight pause.*)

HUNGRY MOTHER: So'm I.

THE MOOK: I'll be right up.

(*Click.* HUNGRY MOTHER *stares at the blue light, still "on". He spears beans with a fork.*)

HUNGRY MOTHER: How long can he keep this up? Three beans, three prongs. One bean per prong, it's only fair. How long, ladies and gentlemen? Stick with me, friends, the suspense is killing.

(JANIS *enters.*)

HUNGRY MOTHER: Like beans?

(*Flings one.*) What's your opinion? (*Flings another.*) On-the-spot woman-in-the-street interview how do you like your beans?

JANIS: Boiled.

HUNGRY MOTHER: Very good. You're right in step with the rest of America. Just another pedestrian. (*Flings a forkful of beans, striking* JANIS.) Hey! Bull's eye! Well, maybe not a direct hit, maybe not *ground zero*, but certainly *close enough for jazz*, wouldn't you say? Yes, once again, that's — *close enough for jazz*! . . . You ought to do something about that bean stain, little lady. Isn't she pathetic, ladies and gentlemen?

(JANIS, *wary, backs off. Pause.*)

HUNGRY MOTHER: Oh . . . yeah. Don't be alarmed. Just part of my standard improvisation avec beans. Nothing to be ashamed of.

JANIS: Are you Hungry Mother? That's a stupid question. Of course you are.

HUNGRY MOTHER: The first.

JANIS: I'm Janis.

HUNGRY MOTHER: I figured.

JANIS: I called ahead.

HUNGRY MOTHER: Right.

JANIS: You said I could come up.

HUNGRY MOTHER: I thought you were another Janis. Different Janis. Janis I used to know.

JANIS: Oh. It's a common name. Not like Hungry Mother.

HUNGRY MOTHER: Aw shucks, that's just my nom de ozone . . . Give it time. The wave of the future. (*Pause.*) Something I can do for you?

JANIS: I wanted to see you.

HUNGRY MOTHER: You're the first, the very first! Hey! Reaching that wider audience! Hungry Mother has impact! It pays to listen! Kudos. Kudos are in order. My first fan. How's it feel, little lady? How do you like the studio?

JANIS: It's nice.

HUNGRY MOTHER: But small. Nice but small. But who knows, if this keeps up, this wild adulation, in twenty or thirty years I'll be able to (*Used Car salesman:*) trade it in on something nicer, yes, friends, why wait, empty those ashtrays and come on down . . . Beans?

JANIS: No. Thanks.

HUNGRY MOTHER: Something Japanese, perhaps. They do very well with that little shit. Transistors, crap like that. Minutia. A definitive talent for the diminutive, don't you think? Tell me, as my numero uno fano, do you find I have a sexy voice?

JANIS: No.

HUNGRY MOTHER: Robust. Virile. Vaguely Mediterranean. Like a swollen sack of coffee beans.

JANIS: No. (*Slight pause.*) Soothing. Possible.

HUNGRY MOTHER: I see.

JANIS: There's pain. In your voice . . . I came to talk to you. I need to talk to you. Don't be cruel.

HUNGRY MOTHER: Rings a bell. I have a famous sinking feeling.

JANIS: I recognize the pain.

HUNGRY MOTHER: Do you?

JANIS: It's like my own. Familar. Similar. Like what I feel at night. In my chest. Your voice sounds like that. That pain.

(*Pause.*)

HUNGRY MOTHER: You're Desperate, aren't you?

JANIS: (*Flushing.*) No, no, I would never that would be over —

HUNGRY MOTHER: No no no no no. That's how you sign your letters. "Desperate."

JANIS: Yes.

HUNGRY MOTHER: Janis Desperate. Jesus.

(*Pause.*)

JANIS: I want you to help me.

HUNGRY MOTHER: People in hell want ice water.

JANIS: What? What does that mean? What is that supposed to mean? I want you to help me. Please.

HUNGRY MOTHER: It's a joke, Janis Desperate. A joke.

JANIS: I don't get it. I don't see anything funny.

HUNGRY MOTHER: You're not concentrating. Is all. Now pay attention. This is Pop Analogy Number One. Rock n' roll Metaphor. You might just cop on to what I'm laying down — dig? You can't always get what you want. But if you try sometime. You get what you need. (*Pause.*) Biggest buncha bullshit

I ever heard. I hate to be the one to break it to you sister, but people in hell don't *want* ice water, they *need* it. And — guess what? They *don't* get it . . . Do you get it?

(*Pause.*)

JANIS: I don't feel good, Mother. I know you know what I'm — I know you feel the same.

HUNGRY MOTHER: I'm asking do you get it. Your asking me to help is the joke. I'm laughing. I'm larfing. You'd better larf too.

JANIS: I know you know how I feel.

HUNGRY MOTHER: Not a glimmer.

(*Pause.*)

JANIS: I don't have furniture in my place. Nothing. A radio. I play the radio. Full blast. Keep the junkies away. They run through the building at night. Up and down the stairs. Fire escape. Rip the copper out of the walls. The wiring. There's no water. No light. They steal the stoves. The gas crawls up the wall. (*Slight pause.*) I turn it up. Way up. Radio. Play it all night. Afraid to sleep. They run through the building all night. Scratch the walls. (*Slight pause.*) I said that. (*Slight pause.*) That's how I found you, Mother. One night. Down at the end of the dial. Before dawn. Strange voice. Cracked. Had a crack in it. Down at the end of the dial. Pain in it. (*Slight pause.*) Thanks for turning up. You were so faint at first. When I first found you. Just a crackle. Clearer in winter than summer or spring . . . No, that's silly, but — my place is right across the park. I think the leaves must interfere? Anyway, lately — you're coming in as clear as a bell.

HUNGRY MOTHER: A lucky bounce offa the clouds. It's all in the angle, sweetheart. I'm 26,000 light-years off center.

JANIS: Incredibly clear. What I am telling you. What I am trying to say. For more than a year now your voice has really made a difference to me, Mother.

(*Pause.*)

HUNGRY MOTHER: Why don't you buy some furniture? Beanbag chairs. Shag rug. Plexiglass coffee tables. Big glossy books. Galopagos this and that. Austerity is salubrious but poverty can be painful. Cheer yourself up. Hanging plants, that's the ticket. Junkies don't truck with hanging plants.

JANIS: (*Trying again, in a rush.*) I felt you were lonely, you said you wanted letters, I could tell, I could tell you were, by your jokes, you were worried no one was listening, no one cared, no one was hearing you, so I wrote, I wrote you. I never dreamed, you know, of writing to a, a public person, a stranger, I wouldn't you know, infringe on someone's privacy . . . so I was really distressed when you read my letters over the air . . . but in a way that was all right, it was okay, it was like you were listening, like you were answering. I never expected you to — that's why I signed my letters Desperate, I thought —

HUNGRY MOTHER: That's the way God planned it.

JANIS: Mother, I didn't mean to write you about me, my problems. I was going to cheer you up, believe me —

HUNGRY MOTHER: Believe me.

JANIS: Oh, I do.

(*Pause.*)

HUNGRY MOTHER: Look, uh . . . what's on your mind?

JANIS: I just — want you to be my friend. A friend. Is that so much to ask?

HUNGRY MOTHER: Depends. Come here.

(JANIS *moves to him.*)

JANIS: Okay.

HUNGRY MOTHER: Tight squeeze.

JANIS: That's okay. Cozier.

(*She sits.* HUNGRY MOTHER *puts an arm around her. She smiles, slightly. She relaxes, just a bit.*)

HUNGRY MOTHER: 'S nice, huh?

JANIS: Yeah. Yeah.

HUNGRY MOTHER: I . . . can't do it.

JANIS: What?

HUNGRY MOTHER: Janis, there's something I should tell you.

JANIS: (*Touching his face.*) Sssshhh, don't talk. You don't have to talk.

HUNGRY MOTHER: Yeah, there's something I should have mentioned earlier. (*Slight pause.*) You're lonely, right?

JANIS: Yes.

HUNGRY MOTHER: Well, I'm lonely too.

JANIS: Oh, Mother, I know you are. I know you are.

HUNGRY MOTHER: Well, darling—as one lonely person to another—(*Pause.*)—*we're on the air!*

(JANIS *jumps to her feet, looks at the blue light.*)

JANIS: Oh. Oh.

HUNGRY MOTHER: (*Goes to mike.*) Wasn't that touching, friends? You heard it here, first. Hang in there, there's more to come from Janis Desperate, much more.

JANIS: Bastard.

HUNGRY MOTHER: Sorry.

JANIS: Yes.

HUNGRY MOTHER: That's my style, sweets. Free-form free-fall. Wing it over the edge and see how long it takes to hit bottom.

JANIS: Jesus.

(THE MOOK *enters. A large man. Elegant. Terrifying. A black Renaissance Prince of the Underground.*)

HUNGRY MOTHER: Ah, Mook! Mook! I'm honored. Long time no you know. I believe you two, you know, too.

THE MOOK: You're off the beam. I haven't had the' pleasure. Seen Free Lance?

HUNGRY MOTHER: How about her?

THE MOOK: I doubt it. You lookin' to get out of show business, Mother, and into an honest line of work? Whyfor you cute, Mom? She's nice, but the Free Lance I have in mind is nicer by far.

HUNGRY MOTHER: Right. Sorry. Mook. Janis. Janis. Mook.

THE MOOK: Enchante.

JANIS: Fine! (*She stalks out.*)

THE MOOK: Whatsa matta for her? The rabbit died?

HUNGRY MOTHER: Naw . . . We just met.

THE MOOK: Mark my words, Mother. The price of fame is a paternity suit.

HUNGRY MOTHER: I'll watch my step.

THE MOOK: You'll know you're in the big time when you find you have five or six half-nigger brats who bear not the slightest resemblance to anyone you ever knew. (*Pause.*) Where's Free Lance?

HUNGRY MOTHER: Changed her name.

THE MOOK: You said she'd be here.

HUNGRY MOTHER: I said I was expecting her. I am. I still am.

THE MOOK: You ought to get out more, Mother. Away from the mike. Clear your head.

(*Pause.*)

HUNGRY MOTHER: Free Lance.

(*Pause.*)

THE MOOK: She didn't tell me. She was going to change her name. She just changed it.

(*Pause.*)

HUNGRY MOTHER: I could use more air.

THE MOOK: I liked Polish Vodka better.

HUNGRY MOTHER: To drink or on her?

THE MOOK: Both . . . *Simultaneous.*

HUNGRY MOTHER: I thought she was working for you.

THE MOOK: In this assumption our thoughts concur. (*They dap.*) Coincide. (*Dap.*) Collide. (*Dap.*) She's not treating me well, Mother. Or herself. She's going out on the limb of principles. I want her to come down. If you snag the drift of my metaphor.

HUNGRY MOTHER: I think I follow it.

(*They begin a complicated dap, a hand jive.*)

THE MOOK: Free Lance. That's rich.

HUNGRY MOTHER: Snap!

THE MOOK: It's a question of precedents. She needs her insurance, Mother, like a child needs her vitamins. And this is a world, Mother, as you well know, in which a child cannot hope to survive without a little luck and some kind of insurance.

HUNGRY MOTHER: Crack!

THE MOOK: She knows I cannot allow this. Not just my livelihood is threatened by her rash and precipitous action. What if my other ladies take it into their heads. I wouldn't want to see them get hurt.

HUNGRY MOTHER: Pow!

(*They finish dap.*)

THE MOOK: Exactly. Thank you, Mother, for extending my metaphor.

HUNGRY MOTHER: Not at all. Any time. (*Pause.*) Maybe she's lucky.

THE MOOK: I'm her luck. (*Pause.*) The thing that really gets my goat, Mother, that really galls the living shit out of me — is that she's setting this whole thing up like some kind of walking 3-D cliché. Right offa the silver screen. Ruthless pimp with the cold-as-stone heart. Prosty with the tits of gold. They get down — to brass tacks. Small-time indy versus rapacious multinational. Victory for free enterprise. Yea. Sheep farmer whips cattle baron. Score one for the free fucking market and laissez-faire capital-ism. Creeping socialism crawl under de rock. Music up and out. (*Pause.*) The record's scratchy, Mother. A bad print. I seen it before. I heard it before.

HUNGRY MOTHER: Why'd she do it? She said she missed you.

THE MOOK: She saw it in the movies.

HUNGRY MOTHER: Oh.

THE MOOK: For Christ sake, I'll give you ten to one. She took it into her head . . . Mother, Mother. I'm chiding you, Mother. Tsk, tsk. In America — life — (*Strikes pose.*) — imitates — media. (*Slight pause. Drops pose.*) Who should know better than you?

HUNGRY MOTHER: I hang my head.

THE MOOK: I resent being put in this position. I resent being made to play some kind of classic American morality schtik. I resent being made archetypal. You know? It gives me a black *burning* sensation behind my eyes.

HUNGRY MOTHER: What are you going to do to her?

(*Long pause.*)

THE MOOK: Ask her to come in. (*Slight pause.*) Nicely (*Beat.*) *You* were close.

HUNGRY MOTHER: (*Brusquely.*) Old days. Stone Age. Before I became the Hungry Mother.

The Mook: Don't kid me. You always been the Hungry Mother. From time immemorial . . . You comin' in loud and clear dese days.

Hungry Mother: Yeah?

The Mook: Right. Somebody's monkeyed with your volume.

Hungry Mother: Atmospheric turbulence. Sunspots. Geothermal radiation.

The Mook: You ought to watch your ass.

Hungry Mother: So everybody tells me. Christ, it's enough to make a corpse paranoid.

The Mook: Especially those Junk Reports.

Hungry Mother: Mook, they aren't for real.

The Mook: Oh, yes they are. Now they are. Every junkie in town, Mom. Every junkie, every narc, every pusher, every pimp. You the *source*, man, the Wall Street fuckin' Journal of Junk . . . Everybody knows you're illegal, Mother. It's no secret. Folks concerned. Highly concerned. There are rumors. Grand jury activity. They might get together. They might *convene*. This whole gig just might go titties up.

Hungry Mother: I can't explain it, Mook. This tube gear is shot. It's cream of shit. It's a miracle it gets off the block.

The Mook: (*Leans forward, very black, very deep.*) Tell it to the judge. (*Laughs, booming crackle.*) They taping you 'round the clock, little man.

Hungry Mother: (*Yelling.*) I don't broadcast around the clock!

The Mook: If only you'd keep a schedule, Mother. They don't want to miss a single spasm. A single spurt. Right now, they trying to ascertain just who listening. Besides themselves, I mean. A demographic sample. To determine your threat extent. It's proving elusive.

HUNGRY MOTHER: I'll bet it is.

THE MOOK: Just a friendly gesture. If you see Free Lance, tell her to come on in. Just like the movies. It'll go easier. Plea bargain. One week only. Tell her that.

(THE MOOK *heads for the door.*)

HUNGRY MOTHER: Hey, Mook.

THE MOOK: Yes dear?

HUNGRY MOTHER: You're on the air!

(THE MOOK *looks at the blue light a long moment. Then grins.*)

THE MOOK: Motha fucka!

(*He exits.* HUNGRY MOTHER *races to the mike.*)

HUNGRY MOTHER: Well, there you have it, gas fans, the heat is on! You heard it all, *live*, from the life of Hungry Mother, a true story. Cross my heart. If you'd like to participate in the life of Hungry Mother, just drop me a card — indicate your primary field of interest — philosophical, sexual, athletic, dinner, dress, or aperitif — and mail it to . . . Hungry Mother, Got To Get You Into My Life, Hubba Hubba Hubba Hubba, WTWI, Frantz Fanon Memorial Tenement, Number One Marauder Avenue, just past Faghag Park. All entries will remain on file for use at my personal discretion.

(*Weatherman.*) The long-range outcast for this weekend — diphtheria! Followed by bubonic plague and intermittent spotted fever. Enjoy. Right now outside our studio — continued existential dread dappled with parapsychological phenomena, and streaked with low-grade anxiety. Speaking of weather, we'll have the latest prices for bone marrow and rendering in a moment, but first . . .

(*He slumps on stool. Silence. He returns to mike: teletype and newscaster.*)

Flash news update. That acute distress has gone — *terminal.* Closed with a rush. Check it out. Other tidbits about our

NATIVE SPEECH

town . . . That dog rapist remains at large. Pet owners — do you know where your pets are tonight? Coming up in the near future — if there is one — heh heh, always the optimist, Mother, check it out! Always the optimist. *Lycanthropy in the Home*! Always a hairy subject, we'll have some tips on just how to deal with it. We'll be talking to a bonafide cat burglar, and you'll find out *exactly* what they do with our furry friends . . . the fiends. We'll also have our Prick Hit of the Week, when you ladies can line up the sexual puerco of your choice and sock it to him — right here in our soundproof booth.

(*Mellifluous.*) That just about puts a merciful end to our broadcasting day here at WTWI, the twilight station with the demeanor that only a Mother could love. We'll top it off with our ever-popular Slumlord of the Day Award, we'll be back after somebody's briefs, but first — a word about *mange* . . . This is the Hungry Mother, wrapping it up here, boss, with a mouthful of joy buzzers and a handful of static, telling you to have a hopeful day, spelled with two ells.

(*Three swarthy individuals enter the studio: two men and a woman.*)

HUNGRY MOTHER: Has to be — (*Long pause; then a whisper.*) *Hoover and the Navajos.*

(*Freeze. Tableau. Lights fade. Blue light still "on" in the black. Long moment. Snaps off. Blackout.*)

[END OF ACT ONE]

Act Two

(*Black.*)

LOUD SPEAKER: The Rising *Pop*ularity of Hungry Mother . . . Beginning with — (*Blue light pops "on", silhouetting four-figure freeze:*) Tableaux Vivants! Avecs peaux rouges!

(*Lights up slowly on* HOOVER *and* THE NAVAJOS, *and* HUNGRY MOTHER. *They remain still, as* HOOVER *speaks simply, in the classic mode:*)

HOOVER: In the moon of grass withering . . . or perhaps in the moon of vanishing animals . . . I surrendered my people to General Howard. My heart was . . . *broke*. I said to him — the chiefs are dead. Looking Glass is dead. All the young men are dead. Or scattered like dry leaves. Or drowning in whiskey. My children chew bark. Their feet are frozen. The old women gobble dead grass and devil's brush. We are starving. My lungs are full of clotted blood. As I said before — from where the sun now sets, I will fight no more, forever. This is what I said to General Howard. (*Pause.*) So he gave me a job.

(*Pause.* HOOVER *holds up a brightly colored plastic package in one hand, and points to it with his other hand, on which he is wearing a black leather glove.*)

Selling these . . . The snack that never grows old . . . Fiddle Faddle . . . That's how I became Chief Fiddle Faddle. (HOOVER *flips down his shades. Pause. Grins.*) Just kidding.

(THE NAVAJOS *begin poking around in the studio.* HUNGRY MOTHER *takes over from* HOOVER *at the mike.*)

HUNGRY MOTHER: Hey, hey! Hoover, fella, you really had me going there. I was brewing up some really fierce Apache crocodile tears. Isn't he something, ladies and gentlemen? We're here today with our special guests, Hoover and the Navajos —

HOOVER: Just kidding.

HUNGRY MOTHER: Yes, yes, just fooling around. Tell us, Hoov — a lot of us — the listening and yearning audience — would like to know something more about Hoover and the Navajos. All they know is what I tell 'em, what I, you know, make up off the top. On the spur.

(*Pause.*)

HOOVER: You got it right. You got it right, Mother. You got it so right. Except in smallest details. No way you could miss. The light comes down on you . . . Smallest things. Our names. My friends. Mother, my companions . . . Crazy Joe Navajo.

(CRAZY JOE *burps delicately by way of greeting.*)

Freddy Navajo. (FREDDY *nods coldly.* HOOVER *smiles.*)

The light comes down on you, Mother. (*Long pause.*) Indians are always silent. Having nothing to say. Ask your stupid questions.

HUNGRY MOTHER: (*After a slight hesitation.*) In the fawning fanmag manner, then — when did you write your first song? When did you first start playing the guitar? When did you decide to devote your lifestyle to music?

HOOVER: In the moon of rising expectations.

HUNGRY MOTHER: In the little magazine manner then — when did you first concieve, and begin to develop as a distinct genre of popular music, *patho-rock*? What sets *patho-rock* apart from other strands, such as goat-bucket blues or cooncajun cakewalks? Compare and contrast. Trace its evolution in a sociohistorical context. How do you account for your obsession with fiberglass? Is it worthwhile speculating along psychosexual dysfunction lines?

HOOVER: In the moon of historical necessity . . . Out of the blue . . . Unrelenting bitterness, as long as the waters shall flow and the grass shall grow — you know the phrase? . . .

An environmentally generated malignancy contracted as an immediate consequence of contact with the carcinogenic substance. In that order.

HUNGRY MOTHER: (*Brightly.*) I see. That's too bad!

HOOVER: In the moon of bowing to the inevitable. In the charnel moon of abject capitulation. In the blue moon of genocide. In the quarter moon of going completely off the wall . . . In the moon of *forced labor* . . .

HUNGRY MOTHER: Right. Got it. That's what gives your songs that grit, that nit, that *sliced life.* Tell me — and I'm sure your fans at home would be more than super interested too — where do you get those boffo bonnaroo titles like *Fiberglass God?*

HOOVER: I got drunk and fell on the floor.

(*Pause. Then* FREDDY *stands.*)

FREDDY: Freddy Navajo here. Earth to Freddy. I hear voices. Indian voices. Mescalito. Coyote. Charlie Chan. Joan of Navajo speaks in my ear. It ain't easy to hear myself think — with all those voices going. All the old voices. Covered here today. Hoover did his Poetic Indian to his usual turn. (FREDDY *and* CRAZY JOE *applaud*) Aplomb. Aplomb. And Crazy Joe's taciturn Drunken Injun is, as always, subtle and tragic. Impeccable. Correct.

(FREDDY *and* HOOVER *applaud. Slight pause.*)

CRAZY JOE: (*Ever so slightly slurred.*) Thanks.

FREDDY: A classic of its kind. You see my predicament? So many voices. A welter. A goulash. So hard to find a point of view. Which piece of history to vocalette.

HUNGRY MOTHER: (*Cheerily.*) How 'bout TB? You know, tuberculosis, Easter Seals for brown babes? Famine? Small-pox sleeping bags?

FREDDY: Hostility is always in good taste.

HUNGRY MOTHER: Uh . . . Freddy, what's the — why don't you do the new single?

FREDDY: Right . . . This is a song I wrote one night while breaking glass on the reservation . . . I calls it — Fucking on Fiberglass!

HOOVER: Give me a ball 'n beer anyday.

FREDDY: Right. Sheer shock value. No other redemptions. Oh, incidental alliteration. A simple tune. Our only aim is sensation.

HUNGRY MOTHER: That's great. Swell, and heartwarming. Here it is, fans, what you've all been waiting for! If this single don't send you, you got no place to go! Hoover and the Navajos — *Fucking — On Fiberglass!*

(HUNGRY MOTHER *puts on the 45, flicks switches. It blasts out over the PA: primitive guitar chording, hand drums, yowling and chanting, screaming, glass shattering. After three minutes of earsplitting sound, a blues-fragment snarls its way out of the maelstrom:*)

HOOVER: (*Singing, on the 45.*)

Fuckin'
On fiberglass . . .
Got that shit
Up my . . . aaaaaaaaasssss!

(*This is followed, on the 45, by a scream from* FREDDY *that's like a baby's howl. During the playing of the single,* THE NAVAJOS *rock out, a violent and erotic frenzy. Fucking on Fiberglass ends with a crescendo of drumming and breaking glass. Silence.*)

HUNGRY MOTHER: (*Softly.*) So visceral . . . I can *feel* it. Uch. Where do you guys get this stuff? Monstrous. Colossal. Curdled blood, see? Destroys me. Primal.

FREDDY: (*Snickering.*) Primordial.

(CRAZY JOE *gets up off the refrigerator. A hush. He goes to the turntable, takes off the 45, drops it on the floor. Pours whiskey on it. Takes a drink. Smiles. Smacks his lips.*)

CRAZY JOE: Primitive.

(THE NAVAJOS *laugh wildly. They seize piles of 45's, and begin flinging them through the air, slowly at first, then faster, to crescendo — a blizzard of black plastic. It stops. The studio floor is covered in 45's. Pause.* HOOVER *smiles cool behind his shades and says softly:*)

HOOVER: *Aborigine.*

(HOOVER *and* THE NAVAJOS *exit.* HUNGRY MOTHER *stands in the debris. Studio light out as streetlight snaps on.* HUNGRY MOTHER *walks into the light.* JANIS *is in a shadow. He stops and stares at her. Finally:*)

HUNGRY MOTHER: Wha'choo doin' out here?

JANIS: Lurking.

HUNGRY MOTHER: Lurking. Huh. (*Slight pause.*) Hell of a place to lurk. (*Slight pause.*) Lurking long?

JANIS: Hours.

HUNGRY MOTHER: And lived to tell the tale. A-mazing. I shake my head. (*He does.*)

JANIS: So. What's the word?

HUNGRY MOTHER: *Hungry.*

JANIS: Listen, I thought maybe — you busy? I thought maybe we could get a bite.

HUNGRY MOTHER: In this neighborhood? A bite is a breeze. But will they quit after just one? (*They both laugh.*)

JANIS: Listen. I know a place.

HUNGRY MOTHER: Yeah? Well. Okay. All right.

JANIS: It's near here. You'll like it. Under Marauder Avenue. It floats.

HUNGRY MOTHER: A floating dive. Abso-fucking-lutely. Lezgo.

(*The streetlight flickers. The light is blue and wintery: a cold evening.* MOOK *and* FREE LANCE *enter.* HUNGRY MOTHER *and* JANIS *stop. Draw back. Unseen.*)

THE MOOK: Ho Chi Minh Trail runs through the park now.

FREE LANCE: Uptown to down.

THE MOOK: Natch. Built that way. They brought it over after the war. Reconstituted it. As it were.

FREE LANCE: What you run on it?

THE MOOK: Scag. Just like the war. Like it never ended. Them good old days. They got a replica of the war goin' on in there. Minature. Jes' a few blocks away . . . Business as usual, babe. (*He turns his gaze on her.*) Back on the street.

FREE LANCE: Back on the streets again.

THE MOOK: I stand corrected. Back on the streets. The phrase that pays . . . I thought you were sick of the street. I been to see Mother, looking for you.

FREE LANCE: I've missed the street.

THE MOOK: I know you have. I wasn't surprised.

FREE LANCE: And the street missed me.

THE MOOK: No, no, I wasn't surprised you weren't there. I know you done with him. I wanted to check out Mother's crib. Wanted to get some kinda line on just what we boosting, here. We had a nice chat. (*Slight pause.*) Mother said you missed me.

FREE LANCE: I miss the street. Mook. Same difference . . . I miss you. What kind of chat you say you had?

THE MOOK: Minimal. I dropped him a hint. Dammit, Free Lance, whachoo doin' out here?

FREE LANCE: Looking for you.

THE MOOK: On the street? Come on, baby. I been all over town, I come home find you *walking* my block.

FREE LANCE: (*Laughs.*) You my main squeeze, sugah. Mama want Papa-san be her first trick. Numbah one, dig?

(*Pause.*)

THE MOOK: You set me up, Free Lance. Like a damn tar baby. Some kind of story. You fictionalizing my position. Dig? People talk. A legend in my own time. Shit. Legend in my own mind. They talkin' now. Hear 'em?

FREE LANCE: No.

THE MOOK: Erodes my credibility. People don't think I'm real. Think I'm the damn Baron Samedi or some voodoo shit. Gets tough to keep the muscle up when they put you in the same bag with Mickey the Mouse and Agent Orange. (*Hisses.*) Know what I talk, bitch?

(*She is about to respond when she hears something in the distance. They both listen.*)

FREE LANCE: Guns.

THE MOOK: *Gunners.* (*He smiles. She shivers.*)

FREE LANCE: I love The Street. I go wandering on The Street. In the back of my head. Stay there forever. Stay there for good. Disappear behind my eyes. You understand?

THE MOOK: Free Lance.

FREE LANCE: I'm not going upstairs with you, Mook.

THE MOOK: Free Lance. (*Slight pause.*) I promised Mother.

FREE LANCE: No, not upstairs. I like it here. (*Slight pause.*) Leaving Mother's, I get a screamer. A rag ghost. I see him all the way down at the end of the block. He sees me. He turns. Gunfight at the Okay. I freeze. He takes a step. Takes two. Now he's running. Right at me. His mouth is open like a siren and he's screaming. He's getting closer. Closer. I can smell rot. He's got a bottle in his hand. A mickey. Like a knife. He's right on top of me. I step aside, and he goes right on by. Still screaming. Disappears into the park. Screams stop. Siren stops. *Chop.*

THE MOOK: Fags got him. Gorilla fags. They drop out of the trees like fruit.

FREE LANCE: Nothing like that happens upstairs.

THE MOOK: Damn straight. I ain't no punk. You have any other adventures since I saw you last?

FREE LANCE: Run of the mill rubble walk. Trash fire circle jerks. Rubble rabble. They try'n come on you as you walk past.

THE MOOK: It's an art. That'll teach you to run away from home. Come on in, Free Lance. Come on in, baby. Come on in with me.

FREE LANCE: Of course.

THE MOOK: Mother's worried about you. You ought to give Mother a call.

FREE LANCE: I will.

THE MOOK: I know you were close. Just tell him you okay. Set his mind. The kid's all right.

FREE LANCE: Mook. Mother's on the rag about some kids. You have anything to do with that? You boosting, hustling some kids?

THE MOOK: 'S an idea, baby. Get all my best notions from Mother.

FREE LANCE: Pimp.

(*Slight pause.*)

THE MOOK: (*Mildly.*) Don't call me that. Don't rub The Mook the wrong way. Call me monger instead.

FREE LANCE: Monger?

(FREE LANCE *begins to laugh, undertones of hysteria.* THE MOOK *smiles.*)

THE MOOK: Yeah. Flesh monger.

(*She stops laughing. Slight pause.*)

THE MOOK: Come on up. Come on in.

(*She is listening in the distance, again.*)

FREE LANCE: Firefight.

THE MOOK: See? Got to come with me, baby. Can't go 'way down there.

(*Pause.*)

FREE LANCE: For now. It's chilly.

(*He puts his arm around her. They start to leave.*)

FREE LANCE: (*Black.*) Whatchoo tell Mothah?

THE MOOK: Heh heh heh. I tell Mothah to watch his *ass*. You blackisms gettin' bettah, baby.

FREE LANCE: (*Laughs.*) Ah, Mook, Mook. (*Strokes his face.*) You're a dizzy cunt. You know that?

(*He stares. Then laughs. Roars. MOOK and FREE LANCE exit. Streetlight flickers. HUNGRY MOTHER steps out and stares after them. CHARLIE SAMOA appears behind them. He's dressed as a derelict.*)

DERELICT (CHARLIE SAMOA): 'Member the cat.

(*They start. HUNGRY MOTHER doesn't recognize him.*)

HUNGRY MOTHER: Cat.

DERELICT (CHARLIE SAMOA): 'Member the cat. Curiosity and the cat. (*He starts off. Turns back.*)

DERELICT (CHARLIE SAMOA): Jesus was not a white racist—as some people suppose. He was the only son of the living god. (DERELICT (CHARLIE SAMOA) *exits.*)

JANIS: You know them.

HUNGRY MOTHER: Who?

JANIS: The . . . couple.

HUNGRY MOTHER: Oh yes.

JANIS: What was that? That scene.

HUNGRY MOTHER: He wants her.

JANIS: What does she want?

HUNGRY MOTHER: Out.

JANIS: What are you going to do?

HUNGRY MOTHER: What can I do?

JANIS: She wants help?

HUNGRY MOTHER: No. No. She doesn't *want* it.

(*Silence. Streetlight out.*)

LOUD SPEAKER: Oooeeeooo, baby, baby. Oh, oh, oh, Miss Ann. Dime-a-dance romance. No-tell motel. *Skank.* Tryst. Tropics. *Tristes tropiques.* Photo Opportunity . . . The House of Blue Light (*Beat.*) Hungry *and* . . . Friend!

(*Studio illuminated.* HUNGRY MOTHER *and* JANIS *on the refrigerator cot. The studio is still a wreck from the* NAVAJOS' *visit.* JANIS *lights a cigarette.*)

JANIS: At least we weren't on the air.

HUNGRY MOTHER: Community standards. I think I'll torch these platters. Do the whole dump in hot wax.

JANIS: I don't think it's right, quite.

(*Silence.*)

HUNGRY MOTHER: Well.

JANIS: Well.

HUNGRY MOTHER: Hope you feelin' better . . .

JANIS: Bye 'n bye.

(*He is pleased she finished the phrase.*)

HUNGRY MOTHER: Yes.

JANIS: You too?

HUNGRY MOTHER: Mmmm. Bye 'n bye. 'S been a long time.

JANIS: Why? Why not?

HUNGRY MOTHER: Out of fashion. *Intimacy.* A blast from the past.

JANIS: I should talk. I haven't been, mmm, with anyone for ages. Long long time . . . Good for the blues.

HUNGRY MOTHER: Curin' or causin'?

(*Silence.*)

HUNGRY MOTHER: Walkin' blues. Talkin' blues. Stalkin' blues . . . (*He lets it go.*)

JANIS: Mother.

HUNGRY MOTHER: Yes'm.

JANIS: Mother, would you put me on the air?

(*Slight pause.*)

HUNGRY MOTHER: Sure.

(*He gets up and goes to the console. Flicks switches. Blue light goes "on". She goes to the mike. Now they are both standing nearly naked in the twilight debris.*)

(*Silence. She lights a cigarette. Drags. Long moment. She returns to the cot and picks up the rest of her clothes. Puts them on. They look at each other.*)

HUNGRY MOTHER: Minimal. In fact, minimal to the max. I dug it. I especially dug it when you put on your clothes. Getting dressed on the radio. It's hot. No commercial possibilities of course. Could be cognescenti.

JANIS: I don't know what I wanted to say. I just wanted to put my voice out there. On the radio . . . What a strange phrase. Strange thing to say. On the air. I wanted to put it out there. On the air. Air waves. Radio waves go on forever. To other stars.

HUNGRY MOTHER: Pulsars, baby. Will the Hungry Mother Radio Hour be a hit on Betelgeuse six million light-years from today? Stay tuned.

(*Silence.*)

HUNGRY MOTHER: Let's do it again sometime.

JANIS: Let's. (*She moves to the door.*)

HUNGRY MOTHER: Absofuckinglutely.

JANIS: See you.

HUNGRY MOTHER: Abyssinia, Janis.

JANIS: Right.

(*She exits.* HUNGRY MOTHER *retrieves his tennis shoes.*)

LOUD SPEAKER: The White Man's moccasins.

HUNGRY MOTHER: Shaddup.

LOUD SPEAKER: Hungry Mother, the Vandal of the Vernacular. HUNGRY JAM! Mega Hertz! Kinky reggae. Rising tide. The ratings surge! He bends their ears! Wild in the streets! Hungry funk! Damp all over! Hard nipples! — HUNGRY MOTHER MANIA!

(*He bounds to the mike. Blue light on.*)

HUNGRY MOTHER: You're right, you're right, you got good taste. Hey hey hey. All systems go! This will be the Hungriest Mother alive, this be WTWI, the twilight station with the terminal blues and the twilight debris, this be a blight and bleary predawn radio debauch with the only Mother that'll *ever* love you! Coming up this hour, Agony News Headlines, something spicy about the Pope, and the evermore popular Prick Hit of the Week. Plus — a bonus. A fab new soap op: MULATTO SPLENDOR! Yes, Antebellum blues! Miscegenation, America's favorite preoccupation! Intricate intra-ethnic color schemes! Ancestor worship and the Daughters of the Confederacy! Something for everyone! Impossibly overwritten! Here! On WTWI! Don't miss *Mulatto Splendor*, the soap that's guaranteed to become a *class* struggle. In this week's episode, Rhett discovers that Scarlett's been 'passing' — and the annual debutantes' ball is crashed by the field hands. And now — *Moan Along With Mother!*

(*He sings a blues moan, minor key. First notes melodic, it quickly becomes harsh, going out of control into sobbing and retching. Subsides. Slight pause.*)

There. Doesn't that feel better? (*Attacks the typewriter furiously Newscaster:*)

And now this hour's top short stories . . . Dengue Fever rag-
ing out of control across Sub-Saharan Africa . . . absolutely
terminal, no, I repeat, no antidote . . . Green Monkey Virus
spreads from Germany to Georgia! If you gush black blood
you've got it! And you're a goner! Isn't that something?! . . .
And . . . the Pope is engaged! We'll be back later in the week
with more on the Forty-Second Street sniper. These are this
hour's top tales, brought to you by Ominous Acronyms —
Ominous Acronyms, dedicated to raising the ante no matter
the pot. And now a spiritual word of advice from the pastor of
the First . . . Chinese Baptist . . . Church of the Deaf!

(*"Chinee"*:) Leveland Bluce Ree here. Lememble! Don't wait
for the hearse to take you to church!

(*Cheery.*) Thank you, Leveland Bluce. Next hour, my im-
pression of a JAP. And I don't mean Japanese. Don't miss it.
But first — (*Slight pause.*)

Trying to get over. (*Slight pause.*) Hauling ass.

(*Slight pause. Then, shakes himself, full-speed:*) I seem to be
wandering today, fans, please forgive me, bouncing off the
boards like a rabid hockey puck, coming up hungry, coming
up short, coming up the up and coming group destined to
dethrone the once-mythical Hoover and The Navajos: Jum-
pin Lumpen and the Juke Savages and their new
blockbuster, *Idi Amin Is My Doorman!* Don't you dare miss it.
But first, it's time once again for — Our Prick Hit of the
Week! Yes, every week the Mother invites you and your
nominee into the studio for a little slug-*fest*. With the aid of
our superbly trained staff of Swiss guerillas, we hold him
down, and you let him have it! So ladies — ah, *women*, keep
those nominations coming. And now — here we go again
with *Mother's Prick Hit of the Week!*

(*Flicks switches. A tape goes on over the PA: it's a tape of Mother's
moaning just previous. As the moaning plays,* HUNGRY MOTHER
*rocks out, finger snaps and vocal bops. When the tape finishes he grins
into the mike:*)

HUNGRY MOTHER: So good. I *really* identify. The weather
outlook is for unparalleled nausea — followed by protracted
internal bleeding. A million-dollar weekend.

(*Newscaster*, à la Paul Harvey.) Top headline . . . This . . . or any other . . . hour . . . slavery . . . on the rise . . . once again . . . in most . . . of the civilized . . . world. (*Slight pause. Low, intense.*) Consider, if you will, the following felicitous phrases . . . Jones. Slud. Double dog dare. Going down slow. Walking wounded. Hunger artist. Bane. (*Weatherman.*) *Thick as slick out there, you better watch your step.* (*Screaming.*) Mexican standoff! Yes! Yes! No motherfucker can touch me now! I full of the Night Train! Hear the Midnight Special call my name! I be full, so full of that damn Night Train! Nothin' I ever seen can equal the color of my i-ma-gin-ation! I am the Midnight Prerogative!

(*Slight pause. Frenzied but quiet, under control, just barely: this is the emotional high of his set:*)

Speaking of *jones* — I got it — for what you've been waiting for — for those with the baddest jones of all — for those with the cold at the core of their soul — *Mother's Junk Report!* Needles are *up*. Ditto fits and kits. Rubber tubing's down. Likewise brown dreck. Something cleaner cost you more . . . here we go! Black Magic go for a dime, if you can find it, and so will Foolish Pleasure. Fifteen for Light 'n Lively, and they be gettin' a quarter for 200 Years of Jive. Hard to believe, isn't it? Topping out at a flat thirty, Death Wish! . . . Sorry, brothers and sisters, you know that's the way it goes, whiter is brighter, and less is more. Now, getting away from dreamtime and down to the street, your Mother's gonna tell you straight. All that's out there is Brown Bomber an Death Boy. A quarter, that is, seven little spoons goes for fifty, and a rip-down, half of that, jack, will cost you twenty-five. That's what's on that open market! The shit is stepped on, Jack, stepped on! Worth your life to stick that shit! Cut with fucking Drano, Jack! Drano!

(*Cooler.*) Active trading in fluff stuff around town: quarter scoops of coke scored easily on the approaches to the park, and it's snowing all over town. Storms of angel dust, methadone in ice buckets, on the rocks or with a crystal cranq chaser, and horse tranqs galore. On the sunny side up, the use of personal weapons in lethal transactions is riding a slight cooling trend — and that's *got* to be good news. This has been another edition of *Mother's Junk*.

(*Slight pause. Upbeat.*) Ah, once that's over, I'm back on the tracks, I really am. Works like a charm. Tomorrow: *Pantheon of Scum*: a grisly scavenge through the deserted cities of the heart. You've been listening to more of the same this last half-century — brought to you by *Sayanora Thermonukes* — check us if your megatonnage droops! *Sayanora Thermonukes* — say goodbye and mean it! And now let's join, already in progress, Sugar Bear and Oz — cutting up in the Cuban Room. (*He grabs his coat and walks out, leaving the blue light "on".*)

LOUD SPEAKER: The *Casa — Cubana*!

(HUNGRY MOTHER *walks into the bar.*)

BELLY UP: Mother! Salud! How hangs it, Ma?

HUNGRY MOTHER: Somewhere else. Give me a drink. Something for the inner city man. (*He downs it and burps.*)

BELLY UP: You bet. (*He follows suit.*) Feel better?

HUNGRY MOTHER: Some.

BELLY UP: Since you're a star, have another.

HUNGRY MOTHER: Catch Hoover's act?

BELLY UP: Indelible. Crushed my head. Had to be Hoover and the Navajos. You're getting very big, Mother. There's already a movement to save your ass.

HUNGRY MOTHER: I haven't lost it.

BELLY UP: You will. Committee to Save Hungry Mother's Ass. The Mook is getting it all together. The DA's hot and heavy on your case. He dug up a diva, and she's shrieking an aria about you to the Grand Jury right now.

HUNGRY MOTHER: What's her name?

BELLY UP: La Mook. (*He snickers. Slight pause.*)

HUNGRY MOTHER: Pays to play both ends of the street.

BELLY UP: 'S a good deal. Immunity from prosecution, all counts' cept murder one, lifetime guarantee. He tags up — spray paints it on the DA's door: you The Man.

HUNGRY MOTHER: He's The Man.

BELLY UP: You The Man, Mom. Your Junk Report peddles his junk.

HUNGRY MOTHER: That's absurd.

BELLY UP: Huh huh. Scag pimps snortin' up a storm on your say so. Ma.

(*Slight pause.*)

HUNGRY MOTHER: Belly Up . . . you think they should sell smack over the counter — like aspirin?

BELLY UP: (*Laughs softly.*) C'mon, Mom. Why spoil a good thing? I'm checking on those kids for you.

HUNGRY MOTHER: Mmmmmmmm.

BELLY UP: Interesting scenario. After they go into custody of the lending institutions, poof — they disappear. I dig deeper. The big runaround. I run it down. It's easy . . . The banks sold 'em. Mook's the middle man. Commission on every kid.

HUNGRY MOTHER: Sold them.

BELLY UP: Into slavery . . . Big deal. Every two-bit banana tyrant keeps a couple of Indians around the house. Right here in town I know where you can buy, no questions asked, retarded kids. Cash on the barrelhead. Watch the tube?

HUNGRY MOTHER: Never.

BELLY UP: White slavery's license to print money.

(*Slight pause.*)

HUNGRY MOTHER: I made it happen. Made it all happen. Make it up — make it happen. I kept . . . talking about it . . . reporting it, you know? Fictional fact, a metaphor . . . sort of true, you know? . . . and . . . and it comes back

at me. It all comes back. Drifting up from downtown . . .
humming . . . the wires have picked it up . . . 'fore you
know it, it's *news*, it's . . . happened . . . Honest, officer, it
was only a fucking metaphor . . . The junk report! The junk
report! Belly Up, from junk I knew from nothing! The
Mook is trying to set me up . . . Last broadcast I did a
slavery newsbit. Just a comedy sketch. Somebody must have
picked up on it.

(*Slight pause.*)

BELLY UP: Paranoid schizophrenia. Classic case. Delusions
of grandeur. Unholy power to make manifest The Word.
Unable to distinguish between cause and effect. Egocentric
cosmology . . . Pull yourself together. You just water,
Mother. Glass. You just show it back. Artists count for
nothing, Mom. Don't take it so tough.

HUNGRY MOTHER: (*Mumbles.*) Bui doi.

BELLY UP: You don't say.

HUNGRY MOTHER: Bui doi.

BELLY UP: Dust of life. Street urchins. Half-breed Honda
banditos. (*Slight pause.*) Shit. I had you lamped, Mom. I
knew you been there. The 'Nam. Moo goo gai pan, my ass.
(*Slight pause. Softer:*) Whadjoo take the fall for? Over *there*.

HUNGRY MOTHER: (*Winks, smiles wanly.*) Fragged the fucker.
Fragged him.

(*He gets up and leaves the bar. After he's gone:*)

BELLY UP: See you 'round, Mom.

(*On the street,* HUNGRY MOTHER *turns his collar up against the
cold. A* PROSTITUTE (JOHNNIE SUCROSE) *and* A PIMP (JIMMY
SHILLELAGH) *loiter on the edges of the light. A* DERELICT
(CHARLIE SAMOA) *stutter dances up to* HUNGRY MOTHER.)

DERELICT (CHARLIE SAMOA): Ladies and gentlemen! For
your listening entertainment—the Latin from Manhattan!
Hey! Hey, man, it's cold! Cold! Thirty cents for some
apricot brandy, man. That's it. That's all we need.

HUNGRY MOTHER: Sorry.

DERELICT (CHARLIE SAMOA): It's cold, man. Anything. Come on, we just shot some junk, man, we need that brandy, come *on*!

HUNGRY MOTHER: I don't have anything.

DERELICT (CHARLIE SAMOA): Man, your heart's so hard you wouldn't give God a break. Shit. Hey, brothers, c'mon . . .

(*They fade.* HUNGRY MOTHER *enters the studio; the blue light is* "*on*".)

HUNGRY MOTHER: Hungry Mother here, it's a fine fine super fine predawn funk — smoke blankets the greater metropolitan area, they continue to machine-gun survivors outside our studio rap rap rap rap rap and the *hits* just keep on comin' — and all told it looks like another fine fine super fine day in this fine fine city of ours! Before we descend into a welter of obscure pronouns, here's the plot —

(*Lickety-split lung-screech.*) SUNDAY! Beautiful Sunday at U.S. Dragstrip Thirty just south of the tarpits! Thrill to the unholy smells and sounds and sight-gags as Captain O-blivion two-time cracked vertebrae champion heading for a head-on collision in his plutonium-charged heavy water under glass thresher goes against Free Bubba Free B. in his multinational banana consortium funny car! PLUS! Demolition Derby! You'll want to be there when the lights go out! PLUS! Hundreds of prize doors! PLUS! Chapped lips! PLUS! Blood-mad brahma bulls released every few seconds in the seating areas to stampede crazily through the stands! DON'T YOU DARE BE THERE! MISS IT! MISS IT! SUNDAY! SUNDAY! SUNDAY!

(*Pause. Cool, calm, very liberal underground FM.*) And now, this week's interview with a Woman in the streets . . . Screaming Annie, dressed in ribbons.

(*Phone rings, rings again. Flicks switches.* HUNGRY MOTHER *jumps at it.*) Free Lance?

(JANIS' *voice live over PA — thick and drowsy.*)

JANIS: Mother, this is me.

HUNGRY MOTHER: How are you?

JANIS: All right . . . I wanted to say thank you . . .

HUNGRY MOTHER: For what? You sound sort of—

JANIS:. . . ah . . . I just . . . just wanted, just want you — I just, Mother — we on the air?

HUNGRY MOTHER: Yeah, you want me to take us off?

JANIS: Won't be necessary . . . Mother, I'm sorry.

(*There is a sound, something falling, a hard surface. We no longer hear* JANIS' *drowsy breathing over the PA, but the line is still open.*)

HUNGRY MOTHER: For what? (*He freezes. Blackout.*)

LOUD SPEAKER: Live Flashback! Live! From the Hotel Abyss! The Flophouse of Stalinism! The Very First Broadcast! Hungry Mother — In the Beginning!

(*Studio illuminated. A tres haute couture* FREE LANCE *strikes a pose.* HUNGRY MOTHER's *taped voice comes over the PA:*)

HUNGRY MOTHER: (*On tape.*) A warm warm welcome to WTWI call letters, and to the station for which they stand.

(HUNGRY MOTHER *breaks freeze and goes to mike. They are both younger, fresher.*)

HUNGRY MOTHER: Dressed to kill. To a T. To the teeth. As she parades up and down in front of our microphone — (*She does, flashing a barracuda grin on every turn.*) isn't she lovely? Isn't she wonderful, ladies and gentlemen? Wrapped from head to toe in delicious apricot leather.

FREE LANCE: (*Laughs.*) Bitch.

HUNGRY MOTHER: Yes, just a vision of fruit loveliness. This is the Hungry Mother, at WTWI, a nouveau station with a nouveau view, on what we hope to be the first of many many twilight broadcasts with you. And on our maiden broadcast we have a maiden broad—

FREE LANCE: Vaudeville's dead, sweetie.

HUNGRY MOTHER: Here in our fruit lovely studios. With us today—Polish Vodka! One of the highest paid, uh, what exactly is it you do, dear?

FREE LANCE: Make it up, baby.

HUNGRY MOTHER: Right. And for our inaugural broadcast we're going to feature something that's uniquely suited to the very special medium of radio: a fashion show. That's right. Ought to give you some idea of what you're up against here at WTWI. So, let's shove off. The First Annual WTWI Twilight Fashions Show. Isn't she lovely? A vision. Simply a vision. Pol Vod is so—well, slender—no, thin . . . cadaverous, really . . . poking ribs, hollow cheeks . . . a dream, really—slight potbelly, haunted eyes, leather boots, and all the rest of it. Wearing a lovely barbed wire pendant, and modelling for us that sensational new black lip glass. So positively sado-masch, wouldn't you say? Deco-deco, innit? If I were to coin it, I'd call it—*Dachau Chic*. How's that strike you, darling?

FREE LANCE: Perf, Mother. Just perf. (*She is still moving up and down in front of the mike, hitting high-fashion poses.*)

HUNGRY MOTHER: Dachau Chic, indeed. Absolutely stunning. And now Polish Vodka is going to do something very *kinetic*, demonstrating the amazing glide and flow, warp and woof woof of apricot leather, aren't you darling? Yes, she's sweeping up and down in front of our microphone—(*In fact, she is standing very still now, watching him.*) whew. What a woman. Sheer Poetry, pretty as a picture. What a woman, lovely, lovely. What? What's she doing now? Ladies and gentle—

(*Hushed.*) Oh, I wish you could see this. She's—dare I describe it? Who dat who say who dat? She's—taking *off* that scrumptious apricot leather—*strip* by scrumptious *strip*. She's—*peeling off*! Oh, my, oh God, oh gracious! Oh so fine!

Backfield in motion! Peel me, baby, peel me off! Oh, my, oh
. . . what . . . breasts, what—what dugs! . . . and—and
now . . . she's doing something perfectly . . .
indescribable . . . with a silk handkerchief . . . oh . . . my
. . . I ONLY WISH I COULD DESCRIBE IT TO YOU
FULLY! WORDS FAIL ME! OH! OH! OH! . . . oh.
(*Pause.*) Whew. Oh my. Thank you, ducks. Worked me into
a veritable lather. Thanks so much.

FREE LANCE: (*Dryly.*) Not at all.

HUNGRY MOTHER: Really . . . stunning. No other word
will do. State of the art striptease

FREE LANCE: My pleasure. Avec plaisir.

HUNGRY MOTHER: No, no mine. How d'you feel?

FREE LANCE: A bit chilly.

HUNGRY MOTHER: I don't wonder. Feel free to cover up. I
hope that was as good for you as it was for me. Do you have
something beautiful for us? Song and dance? A bit of the old
soft foot? Why don't you just *whip* something up?

FREE LANCE: Oh, yes, I've got something for you. I've come
prepared. I'd like to do for you now at this time—my im-
pression of a JAP.

(*Slight pause.*)

HUNGRY MOTHER: I beg your pardon.

FREE LANCE: Jewish-American Princess.

HUNGRY MOTHER: Oh . . . sounds *fun*.

FREE LANCE: Well . . . here goes.

(*As she speaks—nasal Long Island accent—she sinuously removes
her clothes. Her speech, harsh and sharp, absolutely counterpoint to
her sexy elegant movement.* HUNGRY MOTHER *watches the strip,
amazed.*)

I just you know been hanging out, you know? You know
what I mean? I got these like you know *problems* on my head,

you know — I mean it's so off-putting. And if I could just iron 'em out you know, don't you know, it would be *smooth sailing*, no problem, I'm telling you. But it's anything but easy. It has to do with this relationship, and it's so heavy. It's like, you know, such a *hassle*. Who am I to know where it's going? I swear to God I just don't understand men for the rest of my natural life. I mean, it is so *shitty*. It's shitty being with him. It's shitty being without him. I mean, he is such a fuck. You know? I tell him, I say to him, you are such a fuck. I mean, it is trauma time again . . . Am I making sense? (*She finishes the strip perfectly timed on the last word.*)

HUNGRY MOTHER: Very convincing.

FREE LANCE: Felt good.

HUNGRY MOTHER: I'm not a Jewish-American Princess, but I found it as offensive as the next person.

FREE LANCE: I thought you'd like it. (*Slight pause.*) Kiss my vagina.

(*Slight pause.*)

HUNGRY MOTHER: Meshuga. I don't think I can do that on the air.

FREE LANCE: Why not? You're such a fuck. Oh Mother, kiss my vagina.

(*Slight pause.*)

HUNGRY MOTHER: Extend my *metaphor* . . . Kiss my vagina, extend my metaphor. . . . Listening audience, the next sound you will hear — will be — me and Pol Vod-playing chess.

(*Blackout.*)

(*In blackout.*)

LOUD SPEAKER: We'll be back . . . we'll be back . . . we'll be back . . . we'll be back. . . .

(*Studio illuminated.* HUNGRY MOTHER *stares at the phone in his hand. A loud, empty drone . . . He drops it. Grabs his coat, walks into the street. It's dark and cold.* THE DERELICT *approaches.*)

DERELICT (CHARLIE SAMOA): Hey, man. I almost made my trap. Just about got it, just about got it made. Just four cents short. I know you got a nickle. It's cold. Come on, man, I ast you before. *Nice.*

HUNGRY MOTHER: Okay. (HUNGRY MOTHER *hands* THE DERELICT *a coin; he gives* HUNGRY MOTHER *one in return.*)

DERELICT (CHARLIE SAMOA): Here, man. Change.

HUNGRY MOTHER: Honest man.

DERELICT (CHARLIE SAMOA): Apricot brandy. Jesus in a bottle. (THE DERELICT *scuttles off into the dark.* THE PIMP *and* THE PROSTITUTE *appear on the edges of the light.*)

PROSTITUTE (JOHNNIE SUCROSE): Hey, John. Looking for something?

HUNGRY MOTHER: Pay phone.

PIMP (JIMMY SHILLEAGH): Not on this block.

PROSTITUTE (JOHNNIE SUCROSE): Lonely, honey? Party?

(THE DERELICT (CHARLIE SAMOA) *comes back around the corner, a bottle in a paper bag.*)

DERELICT (CHARLIE SAMOA): Care for a choke?

HUNGRY MOTHER: No thanks.

(THE DERELICT *hits* HUNGRY MOTHER *across the face with the bottle. He falls to his knees. Blood.*)

DERELICT (CHARLIE SAMOA): How 'bout now?

HUNGRY MOTHER: Stuff it.

(THE DERELICT *walks around* HUNGRY MOTHER, *stops sighs.*)

DERELICT (CHARLIE SAMOA): Hungry Momma. Hungry Momma. The real item.

HUNGRY MOTHER: Charlie Samoa.

(*Slight pause.*)

CHARLIE SAMOA: Acute.

HUNGRY MOTHER: Cholly. Whatchoo doin' on the street, Cholly?

CHARLIE SAMOA: I beat the rap, Mom.

HUNGRY MOTHER: Congratulations.

CHARLIE SAMOA: I knew you'd be happy for me.

HUNGRY MOTHER: Nobody loves you like your Mother, Cholly. Where's your pals. Johnnie Suc. Jimmy Shill.

CHARLIE SAMOA: At home.

(JIMMY SHILLELAGH *strikes a match, illuminating the darkness.* CHARLIE *laughs.*)

Tuning up their fingers.

(HUNGRY MOTHER *glances at* JOHNNIE *and* JIMMY.)

HUNGRY MOTHER: Okay, Cholly Sam, I'm mugged. Consider me mugged. Take it all. Spectacles, testicles, wallet, and wings.

CHARLIE SAMOA: (*Half grins.*) Sssssssssss.

HUNGRY MOTHER: C'mon, Cholly Sam! Do your number! Run it down! Dissemble!

(*Slight pause.*)

CHARLIE SAMOA: Dissemble. Shit . . . Big Ma-moo, ain't you somethin'? Talk about barbarians, shit like that. You sound just like a boo-jwa-zee. You know that?

HUNGRY MOTHER: Where'd you learn that word?

CHARLIE SAMOA: What word? Bar-barian?

HUNGRY MOTHER: Bourgeoisie.

CHARLIE SAMOA: CC. C'mon, Mom, lighten up. Get rid of that boojwa snide. I been to CC. We all been to CC. All God's chillun been to City College . . . (*Laughs.*) Which accounts for dem rising expectations. (*He begins to stalk* HUNGRY MOTHER.) Expectations which can in no way be satisfied. Now or ever.

(HUNGRY MOTHER *begins speaking very rapidly, as if to fend him off with words.*)

HUNGRY MOTHER: Tell me, as a member of the affected class, do you believe there is a deliberate, that is to say conscious effort on the part of the authorities, if you will, the powers that be, or if you prefer the money men, the movers and shakers, the high-rolling high-rise boys, the fat cats, the leopard-coat ladies—

(JIMMY *and* JOHNNIE *join the stalk, snarling;* HUNGRY MOTHER *falters, but goes on:*)

—to, uh, uh, cut back, uh, basic social services, restrict access to education, lower the already abysmal standard of living and further degrade the quality of life for the poor, in a cynical calculated attempt to discourage democratic tendencies, stifle aspirations, slay rising expectations, and narcoticize anger, in order to escape culpability and social conflagration?

CHARLIE SAMOA: Yeah. In a word.

HUNGRY MOTHER: Fat lot of good it did you, learning that word.

CHARLIE SAMOA: (*Laughs.*) Barbarian? No, Mother, it did not do me no good at all. I shoulda known better. Waste a time. Coulda been out on the street. Fulfilling my destiny as a social predator. My folks, you know?

HUNGRY MOTHER: Is there a pay phone around here?

CHARLIE SAMOA: Old folks, you know? They get sappy. All the resins harden up. They didn't cop to the dead end.

HUNGRY MOTHER: (*Cheery radio.*) They never apprehended the dynamics of racial interaction.

CHARLIE SAMOA: Yeah. They never apprehended the *dynamic.* Anybody can talk like you, Mother. You know that? Anybody. Who you wanna call this hour?

HUNGRY MOTHER: Emergency. 911.

CHARLIE SAMOA: Number's been changed. Unlisted. That l'il girl snuffed herself on your show tonight. That your idea?

HUNGRY MOTHER: Fuck off.

CHARLIE SAMOA: Way too late for the SOS. Is that a first?

HUNGRY MOTHER: What do you think?

CHARLIE SAMOA: I think so . . . I think it is. Now, *that's* a record. Mother. Your best show. So far.

HUNGRY MOTHER: My fan club. You guys must be the new bulge in my demographics.

JOHNNIE SUCROSE: I told you. We never miss a show.

JIMMY SHILLELAGH: Bastard.

JOHNNIE SUCROSE: I be all over you. Like ugly on a gorilla.

CHARLIE SAMOA: Like *white* on rice.

(*They laugh.* CHARLIE SAMOA *is winding a chain around his fist.*)

HUNGRY MOTHER: Is this any way for a fan club to act?

JOHNNIE SUCROSE: I wouldn't give you the sweat off my balls.

JIMMY SHILLELAGH: Mistah Kurtz, Mothah, he dead.

(*They mug him, ferociously. As they do, studio lights up:* HOOVER *and* THE NAVAJOS *enter, in their dark glasses, and trash the studio; blue broadcast light in studio goes out; mugging ends;* CHARLIE, JOHNNIE, *and* JIMMY *exit, exhilarated; trashing stops,* CRAZY JOE *and* FREDDY *exit;* HOOVER, *with great ceremony and delicacy, pulls a white feather from his vest and floats it down upon the wreckage;* HOOVER *smiles cooly and strolls out.*)

(*Bloodied and shaken,* HUNGRY MOTHER *staggers into the ruined studio.*)

HUNGRY MOTHER: Oh, sweet Christ. (*He picks up the feather.*) Got to be — Hoover and the — (*He pulls the dead blue bulb out of the socket and smashes it on the floor.*) Navajos! (*Roots around, finds another blue bulb.*) All right.

(*Carefully replaces it. Nothing. He starts to laugh. Flicks switches. Strikes the console, tearing his hands. Laughter becomes sobs, then screams on each blow. Stops, exhausted.* THE MOOK *enters.* HUNGRY MOTHER *turns to* THE MOOK *and raises his bloody hands.*)

HUNGRY MOTHER: My impersonation of Screaming Annie.

THE MOOK: With ribbons.

HUNGRY MOTHER: Agaga.

THE MOOK: I come to get you out, Mother.

HUNGRY MOTHER: Can't.

THE MOOK: Why?

HUNGRY MOTHER: I'm . . . *estranged.*

THE MOOK: Anomie?

(HUNGRY MOTHER *looks up at him.*)

HUNGRY MOTHER: You been to CC too. Cholly Sam's right. Anybody can talk like me. Yeah. Anomie. It's *rude* out there.

THE MOOK: Rude.

HUNGRY MOTHER: The weather today, Mook, very rude with streaks of mean. Never underestimate the effects of rudeness on the disintegrating personality.

THE MOOK: A little rude, maybe. Somewhat abrupt. Always a little rude this time of year. Gulf stream. Me, I call it brisk. Crisp collars, sharp lapels.

HUNGRY MOTHER: I lead a life of rudeness.

THE MOOK: Genteel. Always.

HUNGRY MOTHER: Rudeness. Covered with dogshit. Tell you something. Shit doesn't increase arithmetically. It increases geometrically. So, instead of twice as much shit, you got shit squared and shit cubed.

THE MOOK: (*Laughs softly.*) I can dig it. Come on, Mother. Come with me.

HUNGRY MOTHER: Why?

THE MOOK: They gonna bust you.

HUNGRY MOTHER: How you know that?

THE MOOK: I set you up.

(*Pause.* HUNGRY MOTHER *gets to his feet, stumbles, finds the bean can.*)

HUNGRY MOTHER: Bean?

THE MOOK: Le's go.

HUNGRY MOTHER: Lemme alone. It's been a tough day.

THE MOOK: Le's go baby! I can . . . *finesse* it for you.

HUNGRY MOTHER: Forget it. No big deal. Been busted before.

THE MOOK: But whatchoo gonna do with yo'mouthpiece shut down? Whatchoo gonna do when you can't run yo' mouth?

HUNGRY MOTHER: Tell you what you can do for me, Mook. Tell you what. (*Formally.*) Why don't you loan me a dollar or two . . .

THE MOOK: So the dogs won't piss on you? (*They both laugh.*)

HUNGRY MOTHER: Outstanding. You know the phrase.

THE MOOK: (*Doing a little dance of inspiration.*) C'mon, big Mom. Snap back, baby, snap back! You my second string. The Mook lookin' for you to follow in his steps. Bounce back, Mom. You can do it. Bounce back!

(HUNGRY MOTHER *lies down.*)

Charp. (*He flips a coin on* HUNGRY MOTHER*'s chest.*) There you go, boy. Knock yo'se'f out.

(HUNGRY MOTHER *leaps up and grabs the bowie knife.*)

HUNGRY MOTHER: (*Very quietly.*) What do you say we engage in a little internecine behavior?

THE MOOK: Stay cool, baby. You can hack it.

HUNGRY MOTHER: Let's go to the mat. Just you and me.

THE MOOK: Don't act the honkey. I found Free Lance.

(*This stops* HUNGRY MOTHER *cold. He stares at* THE MOOK *for a moment, then throws the knife into the floor.*)

HUNGRY MOTHER: Where?

THE MOOK: She came in. I took her back.

HUNGRY MOTHER: That's *white* of you.

THE MOOK: Easy. Easy. Don't press your luck.

HUNGRY MOTHER: Sorry . . . She all right?

THE MOOK: Well, you know, Mother, excess sentiment has always been my tragic flaw. My tragic flaw. She had made a monkey out of me, Mother. Set a deadly precedent. She had burned the goddamn church. To see the church burn, Mother, is to realize you *can* burn the church. Powerful realization. It was incumbent upon me — as a businessman — to provide a metaphor. An antidote. Powerful one. I cannot abide no more fires . . . Of course, I realize I was in danger — danger of fulfilling the cliché Free Lance had constructed for me. So I struggled. I love Free Lance. You know that. But what could I do? There was just no way home. She had put herself in the box. Deep. So I said to my pretty little self — piss on it. Ever cut yourself on a piece of paper? (THE MOOK *draws a hand across his throat.*) Linen stationery. Slit. Gush. *Sharp.* Bled blue, bled blue. Black gash. Mouth to mouth. My hands were cold. What bothered me most was fulfilling the cliché. Predestination jive. 'Course, she could have been rescued. By you. Violins up, violins out. Perfect. And let me off the hook. Muffed it, Mother.

HUNGRY MOTHER: I could call you names.

THE MOOK: Charlie Samoa works for me.

(*Slight pause.*)

HUNGRY MOTHER: Why'd they mug me? Give me a plot point. Something to hang on to.

THE MOOK: Reason? Let go, baby. (*Laughs.*) What if I told you that l'il slit who checked out over your air — that was Charlie's sister. I had to let him have you.

HUNGRY MOTHER: No relation.

THE MOOK: No *reason*. *No reason at all*. 'Cause he *felt* like it
. . . I *made* you, Mother. Don't you dare forget it. Was The
Mook who turned yo' volume up, and nobody else. So's you
could be *heard*. So's you could run yo' mouth. Put it out
there. On de air. You done good by me. I 'preciate that.
Made me a lot of scratch. The bust be here soon. I got to
bust my Mother now — but I sure as shit can still save yo' ass.

HUNGRY MOTHER: Pimp. Scag sum. Smack ghoul.

THE MOOK: Tsk. Tsk. Tsk. Feeble. Mighty lame. You
shoulda held on to that knife, boy. You ignorant, Mama.
Got to teach you all the rules to you own game. (*Tenderly*.)
Come with me, Mother. Don't be bitter. Be my, be my minion. My one and only minion.

HUNGRY MOTHER: (*Shaking his head*.) The exigencies change.

(*A beat, and then* THE MOOK *roars, raucous falsetto laughter*.)

THE MOOK: Keep after them blackisms, boy! You keep after
them blackisms, boy! You get there yet! . . . You know, you
right, Mom. I be feelin' pimpish to-day! Be feeling pimpish.
(*At the door, he turns back*.) Momma — I thought you'd like to
know — I got a terrific price for them kids. (*Roars again.
Stops*.) Keep after it, boy. You get to be a nigger yet. (*Roars
again. Exits*.)

(HUNGRY MOTHER *makes his way to the mike. Flicks switches.
The blue light stays "off". He doesn't seem to notice*.)

HUNGRY MOTHER: (*Into the mike*.) Test if it dead . . . Give
me a try before you pass me by . . . Close enough for ground
zero . . . I've got some good phrases from romantic literature
in my head. It's too bad . . . This is the Hungry Mother. The
Universal Disc Jockey. God's own deejay. Goin' down slow.
(*Black*.) Cat's pajamas . . . This is your Hungry Mother
talkin' to you! I cannot be slow — that why I'm so fast! (*Sings an
offhand blues*.) Goin' down slow — oh goin' down slow — but at
least I am — going down — on yoouuu. (*Laid back Top 40*.) One
of our very very large numbers, I just know you're gonna

love this one — an old old stand-bye, a super-monster in its time — an antediluvian smash — *Sweet Gash*! Oh so sweet! Play it for me just one more time!

(*Frenzied Top 40.*) Get down! As your audio agitator I strongly advise you to get down! Get Down! Work yourselves into a frenzy with — Screaming Annie! (*A series of gagging screams. Then in the grand manner.*) When men were men and rock and roll was king. Never the twain shall meet. Send a salami to you boy in the army. (*Slight pause.*) Human freedom diminishing, even vanishing. Ruination.

(*Mellifluous.*) We'll have the latest up-to-date quotations on — human wreckage futures in a moment. (*Beat.*) This is you favorite Hungry Mother, illuminating the dark contours of native speech. (*Pause. From this point on, the various radio voices drop away.*)

Fuck. Fuck it. Fucked up. Hit you across your fucking mouth. Fuck with me and I'll really fuck you up . . . I try to watch my language, but I'm a victim of history. Or is it eschatology? Verbal inflation is at an all-time high. (*Slight pause.*) First Chinese Baptist Church of the Deaf. (*Slight pause.*) Social engineering. Upward mobility. *Stiletto.* (*Slight pause. A travel agent.*) Vacation in — steamy — South Africa! (*Slight pause.*) Say *hungry.*

(*Slight pause. Cheery salesman.*) Death Boy, Brown Bomber, White Death, Stallion Stick, Casa Boom, Snow Storm, Allah Supreme, White Noise, Sweet Surrender, Death Wish, Turkish Delight! Any size lot, any cut ratio, buy in bulk and saaaave! If we don't have it, it ain't worth having! If our sauce don't send you, you got no place to go!

(*Laughs, then screaming.*) That junk is shit! Shit! Stay 'way. Mother advises you to stay a-way — lay off it all 'cept for Death Wish Smoking Mixture Number 3. After all — why stick when you can blow? (*Slight pause.*) Stick with us. (*Laughs.*) Stick *with* us. Stick with *us.* Stick it. (*Slight pause.*) Twenty-four hour shooting galleries. (*Slight pause.*) The American Meat Institute presents. Our Lady Of The Cage.

A new barbed-wire ballet. With automatic weapons. (*Slight pause.*) Say hungry . . . I'm interested in abused forms. (*Black.*) She not only willing, she *able.* (*Sportscaster.*) Playing hurt. Photo finish. Cut to ribbons . . . That goes without saying. (*Slight pause.*) Dead on my feet. (*Slight pause.*) I pay lip service every chance I get. Flophouse of Stalinism. Two mules and a colored boy. Better a cocksucker than a Communist. (*Pause.*) Down avenues of blue exhaust. (*Pause.*) Voodoo kit. Razor ribbon. Front me 'til Friday. A day late a dollar short. Tryin' to get over. (*Pause.*) Spike that beautiful black vein! Spike it! (*Pause.*) Say *hungry*! . . . Born to shoot junk. Strafe me, baby. Strafe me. Up against it. *Aphasia.* All the rage. Hungry. Riff. On the rag. In the name of the father, and of the son, and of the holocaust. World without end. Shit from shortcake. Estatic suffering.

(*He falters.*) I disremember. (*Slight pause. Trembling:*) Brush fire wars. Bane of my existence. Blue sky *ventures*! (*Top 40 outburst.*) The watchword for today — *hydrogenize slumism*! Bear that in mind. (*Pause.*) Under the gun. (*Pause.*) Under the gun. (*Pause.*) Under the gun. (*Pause.*) Free-fire zone. (*Pause.*) When I get back . . . When I get back to The World — (*Lightly.*) I ain't gonna do nothin' . . . but stay black — an' die. (*Slight pause.*) I'm *serious.* (*Laughs. Freezes.*)

(*The blue broadcast light pops "on". After a moment the lights dim and slowly fade. Out. The blue light glows a moment, then extinguishes. Blackout.*)

[END OF PLAY]

BATTERY

BY DANIEL THERRIAULT

Electricity is the central metaphor and an expressive image for this unusual love story set in an electrical workshop. This young playwright has been compared to Sam Shepard and David Mamet for his superb use of language. Two males, one female; single interior set.

One Acts ~ And ~ Monologues ~ For ~ Women

BY ~ LUDMILLA BOLLOW

These haunting plays mark the arrival of a new voice in the American Theater. This volume consists of two thirty to thirty-five minute monologues and a forty minute one-act for two women. All three call for simple interior sets.